GOD GIVE ME FAITH

AND OTHER PRAYERS YOU DON'T WANT TO PRAY

RAYEL BAUSENHAUS

 FriesenPress

One Printers Way
Altona, MB R0G 0B0
Canada

www.friesenpress.com

ISBN
978-1-03-916691-2 (Hardcover)
978-1-03-916690-5 (Paperback)
978-1-03-916692-9 (eBook)

1. BIOGRAPHY & AUTOBIOGRAPHY, PERSONAL MEMOIRS

Distributed to the trade by The Ingram Book Company

For Adam, Knox and Savvy
- my heart beats in you three.

TABLE OF CONTENTS

A NOTE FROM THE AUTHOR . . .

You picked up a book about sandwiches. Yeah, you read that right. You're going to invest some of your time reading about sandwiches, or rather, what it's like to be *in* a sandwich.

There's this idea out there that, at some point, we'll all enter the "sandwich generation." It's this in-between space. One where you are supporting your own children while caring for your aging parents. This concept assumes a lot of things: one, that you want and can have your own children; two, that your parents are old enough when you have kids to need help; and three, that you help out of love, obligation, or both. It assumes the sandwich is between forty and fifty-five years old—hopefully less mouldy and crusty than I would expect that sandwich to be.

I became a PB&J on my twenty-sixth birthday.

At twenty-six, I entered this club that my in-laws hadn't even entered yet. I gained exclusive access to the world of powers of attorney, diapers, and advocating for someone older and beyond myself. I went from becoming somewhat newly independent into having dependents. Despite all the support my family and I had, it was isolating and lonely. There were no books or resources, and certainly none of my twenty-something-year-old friends were in the club I'd just joined. While sympathetic, they were not fully understanding. In these pages, I hope you find a friend who gets it.

I wrote this book to spark conversation and to create a community of people who just get it. People who are hungry for more than the sandwich they're in. People to walk together through the stickiness that is life in the middle. It's a book for the main characters and the supporting cast of your own story.

This book is equally for those walking through life's ups and downs as it is for those watching others do so. Regardless of where you're at, I hope you find yourself here. And I pray you find a friend here.

What I don't hope you pray for is more faith. People often tell us not to pray for more faith or more patience. While this is my attempt at humour, and I think you should pray for faith, know that praying that prayer is going to require more courage than you ever thought possible. Courage that comes from God and belief in yourself and the gifts He's given you. If you choose to pray that prayer, then make sure that you add this: ". . . and thank You for Your grace."

I hope this story, my story, will show you why grace is so important. And why faith in God, yourself, and those around you is critical, especially when your life feels shattered into a million little pieces. This is my story. When all else fails, please remember that. Remember there are more than a handful of characters here, all of who would tell this story differently. Remember this was the most traumatic six months of my life, and that the stress and worry that came during this time has likely clouded my memory. I went back and read doctors' reports. I scrolled through text messages from that sleep-deprived period. I read my journals. I talked to people who were next to me. I spent six years in therapy with the most wonderful counsellor. What came from all that—all the grief processed and research completed—is this story.

While I hope it's completely accurate, I know my brain well enough to know that I've missed things, but I've tried, in good faith, to tell the story of what happened as accurately as possible. I have intentionally left out a few details, but nothing that materially takes away from the story itself. Accuracy is a tricky thing—what is true for me may not be for others. I want to recognize that the relationships I had with my parents differ from what anyone else had with them, for better or worse.

I ask for your grace as you read this, knowing that this is my heart laid bare on a few pages. Please stick with me, and I hope you'll find it worth it. I hope that you'll find me to be a friend.

Peanut butter best sticks together, after all.

001: IDENTITY CRISIS

I was riding on the clouds, both literally and figuratively, flying home from a work trip to Germany. My thoughts and memories of what had transpired in the week before swirled. It felt surreal and bewildering all at the same time.

Any observer might see my legs squished into that middle seat, but they might not see my credentials: those of a University of British Columbia graduate with a degree in Commerce. I was a tall, shy twenty-five-year-old whose laptop was perpetually filled with draft PowerPoint slides. I had landed my first job at a global technology company, thanks to a mentor I had the privilege of meeting in my final year of university. The job required an MBA and ten years of work experience, neither of which I had. But I brought energy, enthusiasm, and enough inexperience to be moldable to whatever they needed me to be. I was the consummate people pleaser. In fact, on paper, I was an interesting hire: a grad with less-than-stellar grades whose only real job of note had been as a pro shop supervisor at a suburban golf course known for its discounted fees.

Perhaps the real thing that stood out on my resume was this: a former varsity athlete, I was a five-time university champion in volleyball. It made for great stories in the lunchroom but also gave my remote colleagues a sense of my stature, so they took it in stride when they met my 6'2" self in heels. I'd been with the company for eighteen months, transitioning projects and roles as often as the wind changed direction. I was the person people came to when they needed to get things done—I might not have known the answers to anything, but I networked like crazy and knew who to ask for help. And my mentor and manager, Tracey, did everything in her power to ensure that I was recognized for it. She nominated me for awards, sang my praises to her managers, and ensured I received invitations to all the prestigious events.

I was on the way home from one of those invite-only events. Despite my being a company newbie with no direct reports, Tracey sponsored my entry to and participation in a Global Leadership Forum. It was in a football arena in Mannheim, and we felt as much like celebrities as the soccer players who called the arena home actually were. We had large presentations in the stands and break-out sessions in the box suites with sparkling water, flip charts, and abundant snacks. We had meals served on the mezzanine, where colourful bean bag chairs littered the floor. Corporate messaging was everywhere: on the multitude of banners, the ever-changing signs, and the awesome swag given away.

Among the hundreds of attendees were the entire global executive team and ten early talents—the branding given to recent graduates or younger employees. We didn't hate the moniker, but we certainly didn't love it. Rayel, at least by name, was recognized at this conference by the HR folks in attendance. Several weeks earlier, I had spoken at a virtual HR all-hands call, inconveniently at 5:00 a.m. in my time zone. This meant leaving my house for the office at 3:30 a.m. to ensure I was there on time, the technology worked, and my hair was somewhat presentable. Otherwise, I was a mystery to the other departments, leaders, and countries represented. Until something changed all that.

I can't recall the details precisely, but there was a competition at the leadership forum in Germany. An idea pitch, *Dragons' Den* style, if you will. Global senior leaders were split into break-out groups, varied by all diversity markers, including work location. Within each group, the early talents were placed. We were the scribes, copying the ideas generated by the more experienced team members onto the bland flip charts and combining the small team's thoughts into one cohesive idea with which to improve our business. Somehow, my team's idea won the competition, and someone had to present this idea to the entire organization on an all-hands live stream later that very same day. Somehow, I was the "lucky" one.

As someone who wants to vomit every time I present, lucky is very much a misnomer.

On two hours' notice, I had to present an idea that was not my own and that I didn't fully understand while standing next to our CEO and being broadcast to 70,000 people. Our CEO, whom people considered a rockstar, not only had a reputation for being cool but also for having incredibly high expectations. Never in the history of the company had any early talent been on an all-hands call, let alone presenting . . . and not in a suit (which, of course, I didn't bring with me to Germany). The lump in my throat was very, very real.

I've since blacked out the presentation, but I do remember making it to the other side with a fist bump from the CEO, a massive hug from our chief HR officer, and a whole lot of sweat behind my knee-caps. It felt surreal; I was on top of the corporate world. Instantly, colleagues from around the world flooded my inbox, applauding my message, my courage, and, in one case, my choice to wear light-coloured capris. Phrases like "You're going somewhere" and "You're a rockstar" spun around and made me dizzy. Nothing about this experience made sense. There was no logic as to why I became the chosen one, why I was able to rise to the occasion. In my head, I was meant to do this; I was finally living up to my potential, creating a future for myself at a company I loved.

But the conflict in my heart was making my spinning head even more dizzy.

In the weeks before achieving rockstar status, I was approached by my former varsity team to return and help coach. The offer involved three different employers, a pay cut, and zero job security in the form of employment insurance, health benefits, or a retirement savings plan—all things I had at my current job and valued tremendously. The hours for coaching were terrible and involved weekend travel. And getting there was even worse than the seventy-five-minute, one-way train commute to my current job. But it meant I could impact young athletes' lives and have the flexibility to do what I needed to during the day. Plus, vacations would dominate my summers instead of meetings.

As I weighed the pros and cons of becoming a full-time coach, nothing about it made sense. In an ironic twist, logic yet again went out the window. The things that I thought I valued—security, money, success, job title—were not tipping the scales to the coaching side of the equation. Did I really even value these? Or was this just what I'd grown up with, what I'd been told was important? And the more I prayed about the decision, the more confident I became in the new role. The more I felt like this was a calling. Becoming a coach suddenly captivated my thoughts as I dreamed about what could be. It excited me. There was something about walking alongside the next generation of leaders that was more compelling than the way technology was changing the world. Praying didn't eliminate my fears and desire for security, but somehow, it stopped being my deciding factor.

That's the thing about God's calling. It may never make sense in the moment, or ever. You might never realize why you are being asked to move, change, or grow, but as you step out in faith, you find God. You still might not understand. Rewards might be delayed. But at the core of it, you know you are doing what you are supposed to do, which is as fulfilling as it gets.

One of the best rewards of stepping out in courage and faith is that feeling of accomplishment. It was different than when the fist bump came at the all-hands meeting. My head spun. I felt high. This was different. The pride of knowing you did exactly what you were supposed to do. The breath of relief, the lightness of your shoulders. And sometimes even tears fall down your face in joy and amazement that you did something you didn't think you could do. That you were braver than you ever thought you could be. The sureness of your decision outweighing any lingering doubts or fears. These moments are fleeting but can, and will, return again and again.

In the days and years to come, that courage would come and go for me just as the resulting feelings would. But whenever my breath became easier and my strides became lighter, I knew I was living my calling. I became confident I was where I was supposed to be. And, eventually, choosing courage became easier. In this moment, with this career choice, it was not easy but it was important.

Stepping in faith and boldness, I told my head coach that I accepted the roles, the three jobs that I believed were my calling. And I scheduled a meeting with Tracey to tell her I was leaving the corporate world. However, the only time we could have that meeting was while we were in Germany, after the leadership forum, when I was riding high on accolades and fist bumps. The timing felt awkward, and I was incredibly anxious about how she and others would react.

Tracey was, as expected, her incredibly gracious and kind self. She is a leader and friend who cares about the whole person, who will do everything she can to help those around her reach their full potential. We'd become close in our mentorship relationship, and I'd even call us friends while (and since) she was my manager. I confided in her, and she in me. I could tell during our conversation that my decision didn't make any sense to her and she had no idea how she would tell our CHRO of my choice. But I also knew that she respected me, and my faith, enough to trust me. She knew that if I felt called to leave, she wouldn't be able to sway me. She could see my potential in this new arena, even if I couldn't be convinced of it. We hugged, I cried, and I instantly wondered if I was making the right decision.

They say hindsight is 20/20.

In hindsight, I've come to realize that the flexibility that three part-time jobs offered was exactly what I needed. I now recognize that patience from employers who knew my family on a personal level was what my life required. That work where I could just show up and not have deadlines for completion would be my sanity. That lack of logic wasn't a prerequisite to the right decision.

By the time my world started to unravel, God had already set up a support structure for me in ways I couldn't see. He was putting people in my path on whom I could count to do the hardest things, and changing my career so I could avoid the battle between my ambition and my values. A way was made. He did it so that His work could happen in and through my life.

Moving from stilettos to sneakers also kicked off a years-long shift in my identity. I'd always been competitive and channeled that nature into the sports arena. Volleyball, basketball, softball—there was no sport that I didn't want to excel at. Part of it was genetics; I had natural athletic talent, and when I combined that with family-instilled values of hard work and resilience, it always led to success, on and off the court. I wanted to win.

My brother, Cody, and I used to play a game in the hallway in our house. One of us would kneel at one end of the hallway, in front of the linen closet. The other would kneel twenty feet away, guarding our parents' bedroom door. Then we would chuck a soft ball at each other as hard as we could, and we'd get a point if we could score by hitting the opposing door, but below the height of the handle. This game would go on for hours as we would try throwing faster, maybe trying to bounce it in, and eventually distracting the other person so we could score. That persistence to win at all costs—whether by brains or by brawn—took over. I would never lose that game.

Our parents valued hard work as equally as they valued success. Our athletic and academic achievements were praised. Loudly. Proudly. When we didn't win or perform as expected, we got firm hugs and encouragement to try harder next time. It was a reflection of our parents' own lives. Mom was naturally gifted with smarts, and Dad with athletic genes. They worked hard for their success. Married in 1983, when interest rates were 14% and salaries were $25,000 a year, they had to work multiple jobs. The house, daycare, bills. They did whatever was needed to make ends meet. Mom was working toward her Certified General Accountant designation and Dad toward two Red Seal trade tickets in welding and fabrication. They wanted the best for us and worked hard to provide that. And if some financial success and a prestigious title came along with it, all the better. And Cody and I noticed.

So it's natural that I became a young woman with competitive ambition, motivated by money and a title. I had been told my whole life that I could have it all and that there was nothing I couldn't achieve with a little hard work and my natural talents. So as I took to the corporate world, I was determined to "make it." To me, that looked like jet setting off to new cities for work, carrying my vegan leather Matt & Nat computer tote, and walking around with two cell phones because I was that important. It looked like regular raises and title jumps. It looked worldly. This, to me, was making it.

Life became tense. My ambition and self-importance clashed with my values of faith and family. I spent my time answering conflict-laden emails on Sundays rather than enjoying long drives home from Whistler with my boyfriend. While I wanted to spend more time with friends, I found myself pushing them away because I thought they were beneath me, not able to understand the demands of my time and my future as an executive. I gave less and less attention to my Bible and more and more attention to my PowerPoint slides. I craved more money and more recognition. Once rooted in how many medals and MVP awards I could win in a season, my worth had shifted to my corporate performance rating and target bonus percentage. In my head, my values were directly tied to what others thought of me, a criterion shaped by worldly standards of what success should look like.

Every so often, when I'd take critical stock of my life and decisions, it hit me. This wasn't what I wanted. If I truly wanted success and money, then why did it make me cry to sacrifice time with my boyfriend to hop on yet another quick call? Why did I feel anxious when I took time off to sit at a lake instead of networking to get ahead at the office?

That's because my values were incongruent with my actions. My heart and head diverged. What I had learned as a child and emulated as an adult was not actually how God meant me to live. Yes, He made me into a wonderfully competitive, ambitious, intelligent person. But He also gave me a soft heart, with a desire to care for others and sacrifice myself and my resources at every opportunity. He gave me so much, but it felt like I was missing a map of where to take those skills and values or how to accomplish His plans and purposes for me.

So when the opportunity to change careers emerged, it was a significant fork in the road. Would I take the path where I could embrace my full potential as a rising star in the corporate world? Or would I leave the benefits, paycheque, and almost-guaranteed success for flexibility and balance? Could I put my ambition and competitiveness aside for what I believed God was calling me to do? Could I be selfless instead of selfish? Would I trust God to provide instead of relying on my skills, hard work, and desire to win to do so instead?

And at the centre of my decision was this: Did I believe that I was valuable without the title and money? Who was I beyond those things? Two months before, the answer was "Heck, no." My value was 100% based on my perceived status in the world. By others. By my parents. To shift an entire world view in such a short time was dizzying.

Rooting your identity in the unseen is difficult. It means faith in yourself just as much as it means faith in God. It requires work to believe that you are a child of God and that your worth isn't based on what you do but simply on the fact that you are His child. In a culture that values wealth and success, it can be difficult to accept that you need to do anything to be worthy of the love of God. That your living and breathing self is worth more than gold to a God who knows currency is worth nothing in His eyes.

This is a lesson I began to learn as I somewhat reluctantly walked away from the success, recognition, and stability I thought I craved and into a new role. They say hindsight is 20/20.

002: THE BIG C

It honestly would have been easier to handle if she'd said, "I'm pregnant." At twenty-four, a little sister (which I had always wanted) would have been incredible, and it also would have been preferable to the news to come.

My fifty-two-year-old mother sat me down beside her on the ivory loveseat—a lumpy, narrow couch that barely had enough room for one of us, let alone both. Dad sat adjacent to us on the brown leather sectional, with his hands folded and a pained look on his face, like the look that he always had when Mom told him to ground me even though he didn't want to.

It was a Thursday. I had been coaching volleyball a few hours before and decided to stop at my parents' before heading home to bed. I didn't do this often but wanted to that evening. It had been a tough few weeks, and I wanted the comfort that was their presence, the safety that their home provided. Instead, every parachute, safety net, or air bag I had was deployed. Rendered useless.

"It's this, Rayel. A few weeks ago, I noticed a lump on my boob while I was travelling in Toronto. I didn't think much of it, but it grew quickly during my next trip. I went to the doctor and, well, there are more tests to do, but they think that I have breast cancer."

Cancer. The word no one wants to hear.

Tears instantly sprang to my eyes. Cancer. The word sounded foreign to my ears, scratchy even. The completely unexpected twist in what, until that point, had felt like a regular Thursday night.

"Mom," I cried, "I'm so sorry. Are you okay?" In this moment, this may have been the world's dumbest statement and question. My apologies didn't fix anything, and of course, she was not okay.

"Hun, I feel fine. Other than this big lump on my chest, I wouldn't know anything was wrong." Her voice was full of compassion, taking each word slowly as though she was testing them on her tongue, getting used to what might be a consistent conversation in the days to come. Her arm came around my shoulder, pulling my head into the crook of her neck like she had done every time I was sick as a child.

In between sobs, I tried to lighten everyone's mood by quipping, "Couldn't you just have had another baby?" The quip fell on deaf ears, with not even a chuckle coming from either of them.

I suddenly thought to ask, "Dad, are you okay?"

Dad responded honestly to that question. Deadpanned and shoulders hunched, he said, "No, I'm not."

And just like that, I grew up.

* * *

My parents were my world. They were the people I went to with every problem and for every solution. There was nothing they couldn't handle, no crisis they didn't have an answer to. They were a team, in lock-step and complementing each other's skills and abilities. They had to be able to get through this. They had to know a way out.

Rod was born in rural Saskatchewan as the fourth and last in a family of only boys. Even as the relatively "well-behaved boy" in the family (at least, that's how he described himself), Grandma and Grandpa could rarely get a handle on Dad, let alone his three brothers. They were rambunctious, imaginative, and worked hard; the family dairy farm required that. Grandma expected that her boys be able to help not only on the farm but in the house as well. As such, she taught them to cook, clean, and be domestic, which was quite forward-thinking in the 1960s. Dad was an average student, except in English where he flourished, and preferred to focus his talents in the sports world, excelling in track and volleyball.

Rod was the kid with the overactive imagination and was the instigator of much of the trouble he and his brothers would get into. But he was also a doer and a hard worker. In a pasture on the home quarter, Dad and his brothers began building a town out of scraps of wood that were left around the farm. As fans of western movies and prairie boys, they built a small-scale saloon, jail, and bank so they could play cowboys and robbers. They hitched their horses to the hitching posts and used BB guns against each other, screaming at the top of their lungs. Dad often took a horse that was terrified of water, so when they chased each other around their town and across creeks on the farm, his horse would stop at the creek, sometimes throwing Dad over its head into the water. It didn't stop him, though. In his stories, he always caught his brothers. The boys believed they were invincible and that the rules of life didn't apply to them. While this made for epic summer play, it also allowed Dad to showcase his best traits: his vision, his workmanship, his dedication, the ability to defeat odds, even with a scared horse. These were hallmarks for who he would become as an adult and what made him such an amazing father.

My mom, Emily, grew up as a traditional farm girl in another small Saskatchewan town. She was the youngest of four as well but had two brothers and a sister ahead of her. Whether it was to prove herself to her parents, or simply because she was ambitious, Emily did everything well and to the fullest. She was a fantastic student, a member of the 4H Club, an accomplished pianist, and an occasional curler. Introvert aside, she was a surprising social butterfly, a girl who made friends easily and quickly. She could talk to anyone about anything.

Dad and Mom, while similar in many ways, were also very different. Where Dad was funny and soft-hearted, Mom was often sarcastic and stoic. Dad's love languages were quality time and physical touch, and Mom's were gifts and acts of service. Mom preferred to talk, and Dad preferred to listen. One a leader, the other a follower. Mom's confidence seemed abundant in the way she talked to others, in how she led them. By contrast, Dad's sarcastic sense of humour masked a mild lack of confidence. Mom loved to use her brain; Dad, his muscles. Though that's not to say Mom wasn't capable of throwing a ball, or Dad solving complex engineering problems. As much as Rod and Emily were two very different people, they were the perfect combination to have as parents. Whatever one couldn't do or provide, the other could. My brother and I always knew we had everything we could need and more, simply because they covered every base between the two of them. It was a wonderful way to grow up.

* * *

I don't remember too much of the conversation after the dreaded "c" word, but there is one memory that sticks out: Mom taking me to the bathroom. She asked if I'd like to see "it." The big "it" that would come to dominate the next year of our collective lives. In that small powder room, she lifted her shirt and showed me "it"—a lump the size of a softball that sat about halfway up her left breast, where no bra could ever contain it. She let me ask any questions that I wanted, and she let me feel the lump. It felt hard, pulling the skin taut, immovable—a sign of the permanence that "it" would have over our family's story.

I needed to call my boyfriend, Adam. We were just dating at the time but well on our way to engagement. He was out of town with colleagues from work, and I didn't want to ruin his weekend. So instead, I texted him and said, "Something bad has happened. Let me know when you get home." My attempt to preserve his weekend of fun and partying backfired with that loaded message. He immediately ended his evening, prioritizing my emotions over his. He called almost instantly, and contrasting every male stereotype, he didn't try to fix the situation. While I cried, he sat with me in it, let me feel it, with him safely supporting. His voice was calm, logical, and supportive: hallmarks for everything he would be for our entire family over the coming months and years.

* * *

Quickly after that fateful evening on the ivory loveseat, Mom needed to call my brother and tell him the news. Cody was at Briercrest Bible College in Saskatchewan, playing volleyball and working toward a degree in Business Administration. Before she called him, though, she called his chaplain.

"Mike, Cody is about to get some news and he'll need support. Can you be available for him?"

The answer was a swift. "Of course."

Mom's biggest fear in those moments was that Cody would feel even more removed from the family than he already was by physically being two provinces away from our home in the Lower Mainland of British Columbia. A thousand kilometres, mountains, grasslands, and a bunch of cows separated us. Mom and Cody had always been close, and if she couldn't be there with him in person, she wanted him to have the emotional support she would have provided if they had been together.

Despite a sometimes hard exterior, Mom cared deeply for people. Her compassion was endless, and she would have no problem draining her bank account to take care of those who needed it. On September 11, 2001, Mom was working as the general manager of a hotel in Richmond, close to the airport. When the hijacked planes hit the World Trade Center in New York City and all flights were grounded in North America, she opened her hotel. And her wallet. She had her staff set up cots in ballrooms for stranded passengers while she went across the street to a department store. Inside, she bought as many pairs of underwear, toothbrushes, and necessities as she could get her hands on. Her new guests would be scared and without their things. She wanted to give them some semblance of normalcy to ease the smallest of their worries. Mom stayed at the hotel for almost a week, making sure the people around her were fed, warm, and got on flights home once the skies opened up again. Completely outside of her job description, but completely within her humanity, she gave and gave.

Within the week of first telling us of her lump, Mom had a few doctors' appointments that she asked me to attend with her. For a woman who never asked for anything, this both shocked and touched me deeply. When you can see your fears and worries reflected clearly in an almost mirror image of yourself, you hesitate. Those fears become real in a way that hits close to home. Mom and I were similar in our fear that we might actually have to talk about our feelings or display some sort of emotion. In our minds, emotion meant weakness. Or maybe we would open a can of tears and heartache we would never again be able to close. This carefully constructed façade of success and power would crumble if tears were spotted. We were fearful of fear and all that came with it.

The first appointment was with a family doctor at the Vancouver International Airport, close to Mom's office. We'd never really had a family doctor, so this walk-in clinic served that purpose for now. In the oddly dark room, Mom undressed as the resident walked in. After a brief introduction, the resident did a quick exam and muttered, "Yeah, that's definitely something."

The doctor on call then walked in to confirm yes, that was indeed a lump, and ordered a biopsy while they referred us to the top oncologist in Vancouver. None of this was news; it was simply the first step in the complicated web of a process that we Canadians call universal healthcare.

It felt like we had just left that cold clinic when Mom went in for her biopsy, and the follow-up appointment with the oncologist was imminent. Both Dad and I went with her, but when the no-nonsense receptionist told us that only one person could accompany Mom in the meeting, she quickly asked me to join. While the rules could likely have been bent, and it would have been in Mom's nature to do so, she didn't. She complied. And the pain of being excluded from something so life altering was more than evident in Dad's eyes. His shoulders slumped, his lips pursed, and his eyes fell. After thirty-one years of fighting for their marriage, he was relegated to the waiting room, cast aside at the moment he most wanted to live up to his vows of being beside her in sickness and in health.

In the months that followed, I asked Mom about that decision and why she chose me to join her. In her typical pragmatic way, she said she chose me because I could separate the emotion from the facts, that I could handle it better than Dad could. And, she said, she couldn't stand subjecting Dad to more pain than he was already in. I think she wanted to be able to censor the information that was passed to him, perhaps because she couldn't be strong enough for both him and her; she had just enough to deal with her own emotions. In later months, I often noticed that little details, and even some big ones, were left out of the reports she relayed to him. Details that pointed to the gravity of what we were facing. But that was Mom, in control and watching out for everyone, whether or not we knew it.

In her wisdom, maybe Mom was right to bring me in with her, because in this appointment, when the doctor uttered the first official diagnosis in this journey, neither of us cried.

"You have cancer."

There was a lot of medical jargon that followed, but the summary is this: a high grade, invasive ductal carcinoma in the left breast. It would require chemotherapy, surgery, and targeted radiation. It was going to be long, hard, and trying, with no survival guarantees.

In our mutual Type-A fashion, we had a list of questions prepared. While no one had given an official diagnosis to this point, we had Dr. Google at our fingertips and had assumed that cancer was the culprit. At the very end of the appointment, Mom surprised me with one question that we had not discussed. "What does this diagnosis mean for my daughter's health?"

This question surprised me because, in all honesty, Mom never seemed to prioritize my health. It wasn't that she ignored or neglected me—it was more that she expected me to "tough it out." Her common retort to me complaining about my pain was, "Well, are you bleeding to death?" This was especially true on the volleyball court when I'd play on a sprained ankle, dislocated shoulder, or torn hamstring. In truth, this approach taught me resilience and perseverance but, perhaps, at the expense of empathy.

But empathy? Now that was a thing Dad had in spades. When Mom would tell me to tape it up and get back out there, Dad would be the one doing the taping, giving me a towel for my tears, and reminding me that I wasn't the only player on the team. Empathy is something I believe I have in spades, something I was born with, cultivated even more deeply by my relationship with Dad. A trait, perhaps tempered, by the expectations and words of my mom. It was something I would need wholly as an adult, and something I got to shower on her in the months to come.

So when in one of the most defining moments of her life Mom prioritized me, I was floored. She had always cared. I just couldn't see it behind her courtside words.

This all happened in the six weeks leading up to Christmas, including a consult with Dr. Gurjal, a medical oncologist at the Abbotsford Regional Hospital and Cancer Centre. Mom's cancer was something they call high grade and triple negative. In medical terms, it meant that her hormone markers affected both her prognosis and her treatment path. This was one of the most aggressive types of breast cancer she could have. After recommending a chemotherapy regimen called ACD—consisting of three toxic drugs: doxorubicin, cyclophosphamide, and docetaxel—Mom had her orientation and first treatment in mid-December 2013. Warned her hair would fall out soon after that first treatment, Mom resisted, sure that would not happen to her. She was the exception to every rule.

Unfortunately, that wasn't the case. Cody and his wife, Carlee, were home for Christmas. The two had met at Briercrest while Cody was on his volleyball recruiting trip, when he was a high school senior, and had never looked back. Carlee, an aspiring teacher and athlete herself, was the kindest, sweetest person. Easily handled sarcasm. Gave generously of her time and abilities. She was the best mix of funny and serious. Deep conversations were easy with her. She and Cody brought the best out of each other. They strengthened one another and earned belly laughs with their inside jokes.

That 2013 holiday season, Mom was determined to go all out on the food, festivities, and gifts. Dad hopped on board, less driving of the proceedings but always willing to execute on her vision with chauffeuring, cooking, or buying tickets. Maybe she thought it was her last Christmas, or maybe she just wanted to overshadow all the recent bleak news. Regardless of her intention, it was a week to remember. Dinner at the Observatory on Grouse Mountain, a trip to the German Christmas Market, and several hundred dollars of gifts for each of us made it a unique year. The decorations were perfect, the smell of baking consistently filled the house, and new traditions longed to be set every evening as we played a new game.

One night, she and Dad took us all to Van Dusen Gardens. There are hundreds of thousands of lights strung up for the masses to stroll through to really get into the Christmas spirit. Santa makes his appearance. Carols are piped through the speakers. Elves perform renditions of Michael Bublé's seasonal hits.

As we walked along the paths, I noticed Mom running her fingers through her hair an inordinate number of times. And silently, I knew. With each comb of her fingers, more strands of hair tangled in them. She'd shake them off and repeat the process. Tears fell down her cheeks, visible only when the Christmas lights changed colour. More fell. A trail of locks behind her, following her to the future. Her precious thick hair, which she coloured and styled every five weeks like clockwork, was falling out. At that moment, this wasn't clinical for me anymore. It was real. Her hair that she was so proud of—volume that we shared—was leaving her. A physically defining feature was decaying before our eyes. How soon would it be before the rest of her did?

When we got back to my parents' house, I walked with Mom to her ensuite and we shut the door. Together we ran our fingers through her hair until we had collected enough hair to fill the sink. Our eyes never left the mirror, and we didn't speak. We just kept combing, silently removing ourselves from the emotion yet in shock that this was our reality. It was role reversal; all those Sunday mornings of her frustratingly combing the knots in my hair out before church. Instead of her standing behind me and tugging resentfully at my locks, I peered over her shoulder at her in the mirror. She looked up, her eyes wet. Every hair that left her head and fell into the sink reminded me of what was yet to come. It reminded me that our pride was fragile. The strong, put-together picture that we showed the world was covered in hair and tears. As much as we wanted to be one thing, we couldn't anymore. Those locks that used to define the Quiring women would define us no more.

For two frustratingly independent women, doing this unenviable task together was a bonding moment: a realization that she needed my strength more than she ever had before, and my acknowledgement that I could shoulder this load. That I could tape up my emotions and get back out there because this team, this family, needed me in this moment.

003: STRENGTH IN BABY STEPS

The treatment plan took off quickly. There were to be eight cycles of chemotherapy, followed by a double mastectomy, full reconstruction, and then at least twenty-eight days of targeted radiation therapy. Nine months, start to hopefully finish. To say this would be difficult would be a severe understatement. And throughout all this, Mom worked.

Work was, I thought, Mom's reason for being. It was what lit up her eyes, what gave her energy. My entire life, Mom worked and loved it. Her ambition only grew. Perhaps this is part of the reason I thought my value centred on my title, on my success. It mattered to her, so it must matter to me. When Cody and I were little, she worked in hotels. She would leave the house before we woke in the morning, and she would get back after dinner in time to recline on her La-Z-Boy and fall asleep while we did homework. She worked evenings and weekends, climbing the corporate ladder and doing everything she could to join the boy's club of *senior management*.

This was not without a cost, though. We grew up with a mother who empowered us, and a father who was responsible for our day-to-day survival. While she paid the majority of the bills, she wasn't often there to have dinner with us, let alone teach us how to do anything domestic, as a traditional Mennonite female might. She did, however, make every effort to be at our games and events, taking meetings in the car or in the drive-thru at McDonald's after matches.

Her commitment to her job was paramount, though, and her success at work was incredibly important to her. We were so proud of her and what her job afforded our family; she made sure we were financially secure, and the free hotel nights and room service were a fantastic perk of her work in the hospitality sector. She succeeded in ensuring we were never without.

On the other hand, Dad was very much created to be, and play the role of, the emotional parent, the confidant. He was a good home-maker, a great listener, and a man with much patience when it came to discipline and good behaviour—at least for me. It was certainly a different relationship that he had with Cody. But to me, Dad was everything that Mom wasn't. I was a daddy's girl.

When my first period came, I called my dad instead of Mom. A few weeks later, I broke my arm running down a muddy hill by the high school. Mom couldn't take me to the hospital to have a bone set, because foils were still in her hair at the salon. In tenth grade, when I got serious with my boyfriend, Dad had the sex talk with me because Mom wasn't home, or maybe because he drew the short straw. I'll never know. As close as Dad and I were, that was something I wished my mom had discussed with me.

Let me be extraordinarily clear: Mom was most definitely not an absent or neglectful mother. She simply prioritized her work, but the unintended consequence was that her family couldn't be her priority all the time. We knew that she loved us and cared for us deeply, but it was not always in an emotionally or physically close way. As a child, I didn't know any better. Dad was available, physically and emo-tionally, so their teamwork was evident while she was at the office. As a teen, I resented her. I had selfish outbursts over the burdens I perceived to be placed on me by her absence: making dinner; prepar-ing my gear for tournaments. Little did I realize that this was setting me up for motherhood. That this was a gift rather than a weight. And as an adult, I understand. I get it. There's a common saying that "women can have it all." While I agree, I would add a caveat: Just not at the same time.

It would have been impossible for Mom to achieve her dreams in the office and the domestic expectations of motherhood concurrently. Office hours were set, as were game times. Trade-offs always need to be made, and in my now-wise thirty-three-year existence, I can see there's never a right decision. The reassessment of priorities is a daily occurrence. Something will always bend to something else, whether it's kids getting sick or meetings being moved. So much of this life is out of our control. As much as I still wish Mom's balance had been different, mine isn't. Her struggles are mine, even now. Instead, I have compassion rather than a grudge.

So it was no surprise to us that she would not take a medical leave from work during any part of her cancer treatment. Perhaps she wanted to keep herself busy, ignoring her reality. Or maybe she truly thought she could do it all. Regardless, her decision meant we would have to set supports up around her. We helped her set up a desk in our old, colourful playroom, and her executive assistant organized for a house cleaner to come regularly to take a burden off. We set up every safety net we could: anti-nausea prescriptions, wig fittings, smoothie deliveries for when her mouth sores would act up, and extra-thick blankets from Cody's volleyball team on the couch for when she would get cold.

Both Dad and I were adamant that we would be present at every chemotherapy appointment. Every three weeks we would both show up at the hospital and nervously sit in the waiting room, waiting to see which of us Mom would pick to accompany her into the treatment area. It was like being picked for a dodgeball team: neither one of us wanting to be the last one chosen. It seemed like mostly an even split between Dad and I. The winner of the draft would follow Mom through the wooden half-door that blocked the chemo room from the waiting room. The reward for winning the draft was to fetch warm blankets and ice Mom's fingers and toes while she sat for her hour-long treatment. The loser would be responsible for getting ice chips for the car ride home and stealing as many digestive cookies from the "free bin" as possible.

Chemotherapy was harder on Mom than she let on. She regularly told her colleagues that she was fine and that she had no side effects, but Dad and I knew better. Weakness, again, was not an option. She would be exhausted and nauseated for two days post treatment. Then her mouth sores would come in, meaning she could only eat bland, soft food for the next week. She struggled to drink enough water to flush her system, and was often so chilled that the electric fireplace ran, even on the warmest days.

While I won't pretend that my suffering was remotely comparable to what Mom was dealing with, it was incredibly difficult to watch her go through chemo. She tried to hide the majority of her side effects, but her acting was not Academy-Award winning. Her tough exterior cracked as her mouth grew sores, and smoothies were all she could swallow. As her hair thinned, so did her confidence. Calls were rejected from those she often wanted to impress, like her boss. Confusion set in. The days blurred together, and she slept through them. Her mental sharpness dulled as the toxins continued to flow through the IV.

Dad coped by going quiet. His funny one-liners became less, and for a man who didn't believe in the word depression, he fell into one. He would tell me his sleep was restless, and he began to throw himself into training at the gym. He'd do two workouts a day to relieve the stress, sometimes one of those workouts being a one-hundred-kilometre cycle on a spin bike.

Dad began cycling as a way to relieve stress, and then as a way to direct his anger at a situation that was out of his control. Mom's diagnosis. He signed up for the Ride to Conquer Cancer, which was an annual fundraising ride for cancer research that took participants from Surrey, BC, to Seattle, Washington. It was 250 kilometres over two days. Dad was quick to remind us during his training that this was a race, not a ride – despite the event's tagline being the complete opposite sentiment. He wanted to temper expectations of his ability, despite training like it was an Olympic event. And he didn't believe he could do it. He certainly wanted to, and fundraised like mad for it. He trained regularly, setting up rides with his friend Daryl days in advance, meticulously planning out his route so he could look good at what he was doing. When the weekend of the ride came, Mom, Cody, Adam, and I followed Dad along the course. We cheered him on at pit stops and struggled to stay ahead of his breakneck pace. On the second day, we got to the first pitstop early and were able to count the number of riders in front of him. Of the 2,500 riders that year, Dad passed through as the 220th rider. When he finally stopped for water at the second pit stop, having bypassed the first in favour of speed, he couldn't believe his placing. He didn't believe he was capable of such a speed. Dad never realized how brave he was, or how strong he was. Perhaps because he was the youngest of four boys, or maybe he was just wired that way. Whatever the reason, being in the top 10% of riders that day was unbelievable for him, so he just didn't believe it. He asked us again at the end of the two-day event how he did, sure we had calculated something wrong. Adam, our family auditor, assured him the findings were statistically sound.

For the first time in my life, we got to support Dad in something. Mom cried every time he passed, waving his hand at her. She was so proud. Of his commitment to her and this sport. "Yes, Rod!" was a constant refrain while his red and white bike took off down the road. It was awe-inducing, watching their marriage strengthen by their unwavering support of each other.

Meanwhile, I watched the woman I respected, the mom I knew, fade. The things that had always defined her to the world were no longer. The reliability of her looks and her brain was failing. The person who used to kiss my owies and who challenged me to toughen up was in unbearable pain. The person who could work sixteen hours a day, fuelled by Starbucks, could not get out of bed or stomach the smell of a latte.

Yet I came to see that Mom was more than what I had ever known her to be. What had once elevated her to the highest pedestal in my mind and made her untouchable was fragile. That she was human, not superhuman. That in watching her suffer, I found out I was allowed to suffer too. I could imitate her in this too, just as I had done with every other part of my life.

I've determined that there is no good way to suffer. There's no badge for those who grin and bear it. Suffering seems to be as unique and individual as the person. There are scriptures in the Bible that tell us to "suffer well," but what does that mean? It often feels like an oxymoron—emphasis on the moronic part. No one wants to suffer, and it is a result of living in a broken world, not of God's divine purpose for us.

I'm not a preacher or a theologian, but let me leave this here: we have an example of perfect suffering in Christ. Yes, He was perfect. Yes, He was a miracle worker. But equally as true is that He suffered. He was reviled, beaten, and slowly crucified. Yet somehow and despite all that, He trusted. I don't know how that is possible, but He trusted his Father to make it good. To make the awful, the broken, the tragic good.

In those days in the chemo ward, I didn't see any good. I didn't see the biohazard symbols on the IV bags as good. There was no promise that the treatment plan would work, would save her. There was no benefit to the sad looks that came as people saw her bald head. So instead, I suffered poorly. I insulated myself, forcing myself to be even more independent and focusing solely on my nuclear family. Dad and Adam, Cody and Carlee. I focused on my needs and became selfish rather than trusting in the picture God had for us.

I needed control. When so much is unknown or when the fear hits, I get into this "hunker down" mentality. When we can't see the big picture or understand why things are happening, we can tend to create our own *stuff.* We want to author our own story (ironic, because that's what I am somewhat doing right now), where we can at least predict the ending. Because in life, we often can't.

Regardless of my feelings, the chemotherapy treatments came and went, and soon we were saying goodbye to the chemo ward and hello to the plastic surgeon.

Dr. Van Laeken was a soft-spoken, accomplished plastic surgeon who came highly recommended. She was the doctor who was set to perform both Mom's double mastectomy and her reconstruction. On our first visit to her swanky downtown office, we were both enamoured by her style and bedside manner. This woman mirrored my mother in her mannerisms, her class, and her compassion for human beings. Her office was modern, with glass partitions and leather chairs, punctuated by expensive wall art that I can only assume were originals. Dr. Van Laeken was warm and genuinely interested in how we were doing. She had no hurry to her words. As we began discussing Mom's case, Dr. Van Laeken explained the process and recovery for a double mastectomy and then made a startling statement: "Go to that drawer over there and pull out whatever size boobs you think you want."

Mom and I looked at each other. *Did she just say that?*

She laughed and clarified, "In that drawer are all the different sizes of silicone implants. Go, pick them up, feel them, and see which size you might like to be when this is all said and done with."

Who knew that you could pick your boob size this way? A drawer full of boobs? It felt like a McDonald's drive-thru, and in the moment, sheer hilarity ensued. It was absurd and completely unexpected. Mom and I couldn't stop laughing as we both picked up implants of various sizes and put them in our bras to see how they would fit. Dr. Van Laeken gave us so much grace and time as we eventually calmed down enough to decide on the size and feel of Mom's new chest.

What was not as funny were the actual procedures for the mastectomy and reconstruction. Mom struggled for breath coming out of anesthesia after the surgery, so her time in recovery was much longer than expected. Then her drainage tubes became sore and infected when she returned home. She couldn't stand by herself and needed to be propped up in particular ways in bed, pillows supporting her in the strangest positions.

Then began the radiation treatment, a daily trek to the Abbotsford Hospital to have targeted radiation on her chest and surrounding lymph nodes. While Mom's only physical side effect of the radiation was an itchy sunburn on her chest, her biggest side effect was a loss of what she viewed as "productive" time. Her meeting schedule was in upheaval and she regularly complained of her lack of productivity because of her treatments. But she persisted.

It seems ridiculous to describe what was eight months of our lives into a few short pages. In hindsight, the days seemed mundane and marked only by appointments and treatment times.

We learned about the medical system, how to navigate it, and the processes that were in play behind the nurses' desk. We discovered the complex world that is cancer treatment. There were players like social workers and charge nurses who could make things happen that seemed like miracles. We discovered that insurance benefits cover things like wigs and "breast prostheses," which made things financially more bearable for my parents. We learned where the free parking lots were and how to wrangle cheaper parking rates in the close lots.

Beyond the logistics of hospitals, we learned strength—the little moments of courage that added up to big ones. The slow steps into the chemo ward on that first day made the larger leaps into the surgical rooms easier. The worry we had over early scans seemed pale in comparison to the later anxiety around chemotherapy and radiation. The strength we earned, we kept. And the strength we kept, we built on. Our strength started in baby steps.

004: A HERITAGE OF COMMITMENT

Just after Mom's initial diagnosis in January 2014, I said "yes" to accepting a new family as my own when Adam proposed. In all reality, I'd accepted them and they'd accepted me many years before that, but we made it formal with a gorgeous diamond ring early that year.

Rarely do you see arranged marriages in twenty-first century, Canadian Mennonite culture, but I firmly believe ours was one of them. Emily Isaak and Bonnie Friesen were college roommates at Bethany Bible School in Saskatchewan and then proceeded to move their roommatehood to Calgary to attend the Southern Alberta Institute of Technology together as well. While these two women were best of friends, they were, in some ways, very different. Emily was driven to be an accountant, to earn her father's respect and achieve some wealth along the way. She knew how to make warenike, drive a tractor, and can every fruit and vegetable in the garden. Her hands would glide over the ivory keys of the family piano or work the Singer sewing machine. She embraced every aspect of what a hard-working farm daughter could be, and she also craved the respect of her dad, which she felt she had to earn by making something of herself in the world. Her innate desire to care for every person she came into contact with was regularly in conflict with her desire to succeed by some sort of external measuring stick to achieve validation.

Bonnie also grew up in a traditional Mennonite family in Abbotsford, BC, with strong gender roles and expectations of hard work. She loved family, friends, and her animals; and while her parents didn't have a farm by the same definition that the Isaaks did—as in the Friesens raised animals rather than farming land—Bonnie worked summers in her family business. She was pragmatic, choosing to get a job via Bible school and secretarial school as opposed to a full degree. Like Emily, Bonnie cared deeply for all those around her. Bonnie's priorities never wavered: family, then career. She was full in her faith, strong in her opinions, and loyal to her friends. Bonnie followed Em wherever she went; and Bonnie's parents were more than happy to support the friendship where they saw equal parts stability as fun. Bon and Em would come to rely on each other so deeply to balance each other out. They were the yin to the other's yang.

On their first day in the Bethany Bible School cafeteria line, these two youngest siblings became the best of friends and, eventually, each other's maids of honour. They melded together and never looked back. They were two halves of the same coin. Their friendship continued as Bonnie moved back to British Columbia after graduation, and Emily went back to Saskatchewan to marry her farmer fiancé, Rod Quiring. Eventually, Rod and Emily brought us to BC, and the two women and their families remained as close as ever.

It had to be that Bonnie's son, Adam, would eventually take a liking to Emily's daughter, me. Despite our teenage, online romance ending as quickly as it started, our families continued to get together every Christmas for dinner and throughout the year for family game nights. And the unconditional support that Bonnie's parents showed to Emily extended to me as her daughter.

But then something shifted during our regular family Christmas party of 2011. Adam was no longer the short, scrawny high school boy he had once been. He was a man with a new truck and a new job. He remembered my favourite beer all night long and made me laugh without trying. So obviously, twenty-two-year-old me started flirting like crazy that evening, and Adam—well, he ignored it. I'd get close to him, and he'd move away. I'd make a joke. He wouldn't laugh. My tried-and-true moves were useless against this guy—I had no idea what was happening.

We didn't chat again until April 2012, when he attended my brother's wedding reception. While Cody and my now sister-in-law, Carlee, had gotten married a few months earlier, we were having a reception in BC so all of our family and friends who couldn't attend the wedding could celebrate together. As Cody and Mom worked on a seating chart, he casually asked, "Rayel, can you sit next to Adam, because he won't know anybody else?"

Without a thought, I replied, "Sure!" Twenty-three years of friendship meant that hanging out with Adam was always easy, even if the flirting would go nowhere.

At the reception, we chatted all night. He ate my entire dinner because I lied, saying that I wasn't hungry. He was looking at my risotto so longingly that I felt rude keeping it for myself. And during a particularly emotional moment in the wedding slideshow, his arm found its way around my shoulders. We made plans to hang out again in a few weeks, and that felt like the end of that.

Except it wasn't. It was the start of something amazing. We messaged non-stop for a few weeks while I was in El Salvador on a Habitat for Humanity build, and he was in the Dominican Republic with his family. The boy I'd always known to be kind, funny, and down to earth was proving to be a man of character, who loved his family deeply, and who could make any situation positive. One of the perks of knowing someone for your whole life is that the basics are understood when you get to this point in a relationship. Now we had the freedom to dig into the deep stuff, the hard stuff, the secret stuff. People flocked to Adam because he made them feel seen, and he took his faith and commitments more seriously than anyone I had ever met.

Needless to say, we dated, and within six weeks of being together, we knew we would get married. Our relationship was easy, it was fun, and it was deep. It felt accelerated because we knew the surface stuff already. But there was one hurdle we still had to get over in our early days together.

"Auntie Bonnie," I started as I helped her prepare dinner one day.

She interrupted quickly. "Rayel, if you are going to hold my son's hand in public, you probably shouldn't be calling me 'auntie' anymore."

Fair point.

Adam and I dated for a year and a half before he proposed on a beautiful winter morning. Actually, he proposed three times. The first time, he took me on a surprise date back to the restaurant where we'd had my brother's wedding reception. He'd thoughtfully called ahead and special-ordered the same risotto and wine we had shared on that reception night. We had beautiful conversation, and once dinner was over, he took my hand in his, and we walked toward the pier in Fort Langley. The fog was settling in on that cold night, and as we stopped on the pier to kiss, Adam's face turned serious. He began slowly. "Rayel, you are the most beautiful person I have ever met. You are wonderful, and I love you so much. I have a very important question to ask you."

Sweat stung my freshly shaved armpits, and my knees started trembling. I waited. Adam knelt and began to tie his shoe. As he looked up at me from his knee, his smile got bigger and he asked that very important question.

"Do you want to go grab a coffee?"

My adrenalin wound down four gears, and now I wasn't just shaking from what I thought would be a proposal. I was mad! How could he get my hopes up like that? He'd never intended to propose. He wanted to mess with me.

The next weekend, Adam asked if we could do a breakfast date on Saturday morning because I had to coach volleyball that evening. I quickly agreed, and he showed up at my townhouse bright and early on another gorgeous winter morning. As I hopped into his truck, he handed me a folded-up piece of paper. It was a clue, the first of eight or so on a scavenger hunt. It took us to breakfast in White Rock, at the Boathouse overlooking the ocean. We proceeded with the scavenger hunt, up and down the quiet White Rock strip. The final clue led us to a large rock on the beach, where we'd had our first kiss almost two years before. On that rock was a picnic blanket, flowers, and a small cooler. Music was playing in the background, and it was the perfect place to sit and enjoy each other and the gorgeous morning. The first thought that came to my mind when I saw this was, *He can't kneel on this rock. How is he going to propose?* My hesitation proved accurate as, after some more wonderful conversation, we walked back to the truck to go home, with a diamond nowhere in sight.

"So did you think I was going to propose?" Adam teased as we drove back home.

"Yeah, of course I did. But where were you going to kneel?" I responded as I playfully punched his shoulder. We both chuckled at this infuriating game he was playing of "Will he propose today or won't he?"

He parked in my driveway, we both got out of the truck, and I went to unlock the door. As I looked in the little window at the top of that blue front door, I saw candles, lit and lining the stairs. I missed his best friend's vehicle parked outside.

"What did you do?" I asked him nervously.

"Go on in," he whispered.

I went in, and on each step leading from the front door to my kitchen was a candle, a picture, and a note describing one reason this amazing man loved me. Some were serious, some made us laugh, but most of all, each photo reminded me of all the amazing memories we'd created in the last eighteen months. As I rounded the top of the stairs, flowers, raspberries, and chocolate covered my kitchen table. *This has to be it, right?*

Sure enough, Adam reached behind a vase to pick up the ring, knelt yet again, and started in on the speech. To be honest, I can't recall any of his romantic words. What I do remember is staring at him, thinking that this wasn't a surprise and that this was exactly where I was supposed to be, with this man, at this time. Overwhelmed with tears, instead of saying yes, I nodded.

"So is that a yes?" he asked again.

"Yes!"

I chose to say yes to Adam because of who he had always been, but also who he could be. He had always been a man of character and integrity, a man who put everyone else first and who made decisions with thoughtfulness and compassion. Someone generous with his time, money, and ideas. I'd found in Adam a man who loved wholly, unabashedly, and without reservation. I knew all of this about him, and the timing of his proposal was just one example of the core of who he is.

You see, Adam had been planning to propose in December 2013, not in January 2014, so that my brother could be around to celebrate with us during the Christmas season. But when the diagnosis came, he put his plans on hold. He prioritized my family, sacrificing his desire to put a ring on my finger at a certain time.

And that's what marriage is at its core. Marriage is a sacrifice. A choice, a decision, to trust when it's hard. To trust each other's love, commitment, and character. It's a decision to accept all of each other and our circumstances. So when that "something" happened in December, Adam chose to trust me and trust us that we could recover and would be stronger than ever. It's why, in October of that same year, our vows sounded like this.

* * *

Today we stand face to face, in front of all of our family and friends, on the most significant day of our lives. Deep down we have known that we have loved each other since the age of nine, and today I, Adam Bausenhaus get to make a lifelong commitment to take you, Rayel to be my wedded wife. You are my ally in mischief. You are my teammate as challenges arise. You give the best hugs whenever I need them most. You are absolutely gorgeous 100% of the time. You are the most caring person I know to everyone and anyone. You pursue God with your whole heart. You are my bestest friend. But most importantly, you are the love of my life. We know marriage will not easy and that we will have trials that seem insurmountable, but I vow to never leave you when life seems too hard. I promise to help guide and direct you by looking to God first. I promise to be your partner in sickness and in health. I pledge you my continual faithfulness. I promise to always love you unconditionally with my hand and my heart. All these things I vow to keep true for forever and a little bit more.

* * *

Adam, you are my past, my present, and as of today, my future. About three months into dating, I convinced you to travel with me to Saskatchewan in winter, and it was in that moment that I knew how much you loved me. Who else would go to -25 Celsius willingly? In those three days, I saw what life would be like with you, a man who values family, who will do anything he can to bring joy to those around him, and who goes out of his way to serve others. After that weekend, I knew that I was not just dating my best friend, but that I was ready to marry the love of my life. You really are a man after God's own heart. You have faith even in the toughest of times, and you entrust God with every piece of your life. You are kind, patient, and understanding. You give of yourself and sacrifice to make life better for others. You desire to mentor, to teach, and to train others to be young men and women of Christ. You are humble, generous, forgiving, quick to laugh, and you live in joy. You protect, trust, and love without failing. Adam, today in front of our family and friends, I promise to put God first in my life, our marriage, and our family. I give to you my love and faithfulness. I promise to pray for you, even when it is hard. I promise to be your teammate, in the wins and the losses of life. I promise to care for you and comfort you in any way I can. I will laugh with you, cry with you, and watch football with you. I will respect you as the head of our house and walk with you in every adventure we take in life, never leaving your side. I promise to support you, dream with you, and to be strong when you can't. I will be a wife you can be proud of, and I promise to love you every day, for forever and a little while.

* * *

As the next several years unfolded, our commitment to each other and these vows would be tested in ways we had never dreamed. While we never came back to the specific words that we said out loud that day in front of 160 of our closest friends and family, we lived out the sentiment each and every day. The history we had between our families and the foundation we had built together was strong and unshakable. It's what kept us going, what kept us together after the newlywed bliss came to an abrupt end.

A million things could have torn us apart, could have broken the vows we made. But we chose to stay, to fight for what we wanted and what we believed God created for us. Many talk about the fight for relationships and how hard it is to stay together, but I believe it's not the fight that's the hardest part. The part that requires the most courage, the most bravery, is the choice to try. It would be easier to give up, to not even start. To choose each other every day? That's bravery. It means laying yourself down, deferring to the other person, and putting their needs above your own. That's the foundation of love and respect, of what godly marriage looks like. And this would be the foundation that would remain as we walked together over the next few years. Adam promised he would never leave me, even when life got too hard. He held true to his word, despite every circumstance making life feel too difficult.

005: STRENGTH IN NUMBERS

It was a gorgeous February day, and for one of the first times since getting married, I was at an event with "Adam's friends" without him being there. We'd only been married since the October before. This was a casual lunch after church—sandwiches at our friend's house. No one really knew that it was my birthday, and that was okay. I don't like being the centre of attention at the best of times, let alone when I don't have someone to deflect to like Adam.

I texted Dad as I left lunch. "Still on for a fire tonight?" The sun was shining, and all I wanted for my birthday was a fire and s'mores in Mom and Dad's back yard.

My phone buzzed. I was driving to my in-laws to say a quick hi. I couldn't answer the call because my 2001 VW Golf was less than equipped for Bluetooth, or even CDs. It buzzed again. Still, I didn't respond. Then a text came through from the same number.

"Hi, Rayel. This is Cpl Neumann from the Langley RCMP. You sent a text to a friend. That friend had an accident and we do not know his name. Please call me immediately."

Hyperventilating, I immediately returned the call.

"Hello, this is Corporal Neumann with the Langley RCMP. Who am I talking to?"

"This is Rayel," I answered slowly, not sure what the police could possibly be calling about.

"And what's your relationship to the person you just texted about a fire?"

"That's my dad. Why do you know about that?" Bewildered, my head ran through every scenario that could possibly lead to the authorities getting a hold of and into Dad's locked phone.

"I'm sorry to tell you that your dad has been in an accident. He's on his way to the hospital right now."

Tears instantly sprang to my eyes, and my throat started closing, but my brain was still functional. "This isn't really the RCMP, is it? This is a terrible joke."

"No," he replied calmly. "This is Corporal Neumann. I can give you the number of my supervisor with the RCMP if you want to verify who I am."

Oh my god, I thought.

"What?! Are you serious? What happened to my dad? Does my mom know?" My thoughts were moving at lightning speed, yet none struck as rational.

"He was biking around Derby Reach, and they believe he had a heart attack. He fell off his bike and is being transported to Royal Columbian unconscious. You are the only person we have contacted."

"Holy crap. Holy crap. Daddddd!" My voice sounded like a toddler's, scared by a nightmare and waiting for their parent to hold them close. To let them know it wasn't real.

"Rayel, can you get home? I can send a car to come and get you," Corporal Neumann offered.

Not breathing, I responded, "I'm okay. I'll figure it out. I'll call my mom. My in-laws will help me get home."

"Okay, we'll be at your townhouse, and we'll stay there until you get back."

How in the world had they worked out where I lived?

I ran inside Bonnie's house, struggling for breath and barely able to get my words out. Somehow, she and my father-in-law, Kurt, worked out that something had happened to Dad.

Instantly, they sprang into action. Kurt grabbed his keys, and Bonnie shepherded me to the SUV. My rule-following father-in-law was about to shatter every preconceived notion I had about him. In record time, and breaking every speed limit in Abbotsford, he got me back to my townhouse in Langley, where three police cars and my mom were waiting.

Mom was waiting there because I had called her. As Kurt drove us home, I dialled my speed dial 3: Mom.

"Hey, Mom."

"Hi, Rayel. Where are you?"

"Do you know where Dad is?"

"Yeah, he's out for a bike ride. He left a little while ago."

My voice caught, and I purposefully took a deep breath. "No, he's not, Mom. He's in the hospital. He collapsed around Derby Reach, and the paramedics brought him to Royal Columbian."

She didn't even pause. "No, he's on a bike ride. Are you sure that was him?"

"Yeah, Mom. The police called me, and they're waiting at my house. Kurt's bringing me home now, and they're going to meet us at my place."

In a surprisingly calm voice, she clearly said, "I'll meet you there. I'll call Daryl. He'll know what to do."

And just like that, she hung up the phone.

It was always that way with Mom. Emotions hit, whether positive or negative, and she would shut down. Or hang up the phone, in this case.

A prime example of this happened when I was seventeen years old. I was living for the summer with my friend and her mom in an apartment in Vancouver while we trained with Team BC at the University of British Columbia. It was an intense, three-week training camp that included multiple hours in the gym each day. We were left physically exhausted and, after dealing with other seventeen-year-old girls all day, emotionally taxed at the end of the camp. The web of emotions and hormones from fourteen teenagers is complex enough to begin with. Then add in competition for starting spots, gossiping about coaches and cute boys walking down the hallway during practices—it was tiring.

So when I called Mom to vent and talk through the emotions I was feeling, she shut me down. She told me I needed to drink more water and that I was being irrational. She used the word "crazy." My teenage self needed a confidante, and she saw a teenage girl stewing in drama. She quickly ended the phone call, and I ran to my friend's mom, sobbing and hugging her, willing her to be the mother I so desperately needed at that moment. She sat there, stroked my hair, and listened. She didn't offer advice, and she didn't rationalize away my feelings. She was present, and even if she didn't understand, she pretended she did. She was the soft-hearted, best-friend mother I had imagined I would have and never received.

My mother had many skills, but what I needed at that moment— kindness, empathy, and listening—was not evident. When the emotions got too big, she would shut them down, whether out of fear or as a way of protecting herself.

So it was no surprise that she hung up on me.

When we got home, Corporal Neumann and our family friend, Daryl Edwards, greeted me in the driveway. They showed me Dad's bike and his helmet, the side of which was shattered. I imagined him lying with blood all over him, paramedics doing CPR and crushing his chest. Lifeless. In my mind, I saw him die. All this catastrophizing from a helmet. A necessary device that is supposed to keep you safe was broken. I wasn't sure if it had done its job in protecting Dad, but the state of his safety equipment mirrored exactly how I felt. Crushed. My father, who always protected me, was as destroyed as his helmet. It was an irony of the saddest proportions.

The police who waited at my townhouse gave me the details. He had fallen nine kilometres from home, in a popular area where there were plenty of people walking and cycling who had heard him fall. Within seconds of his falling off his bike, there was an off-duty lifeguard and firefighter providing CPR. He wasn't breathing for twelve minutes while they waited for the ambulance to arrive. Later, we would learn that even when the advanced life support paramedics arrived, they defibrillated him three times—one more than protocol states—before they got a pulse. Immediately, they rushed him to Royal Columbian Hospital.

As I look back on this story, I see glimpses of God. I see His hand at work and His plans in place. How did an off-duty firefighter and lifeguard just happen to be in the right spot to provide CPR? How did the brother of a family friend end up being the attending paramedic, breaking protocol to shock him one more time and save his life? How did this happen on a beautiful day, when so many people were out and about to see him fall?

Honestly, I can't remember how we got to Royal Columbian: who drove, how fast, or where we parked. I remember walking in the entrance, head swivelling to find a sign to tell us where to go. Instead, my eyes landed on an angel. He'd love being called an angel. It was Daryl, holding coffee in his hands, but the drink was what we not-so-affectionately called "Tim Horton's swill." He must have been panicked too, because in any other setting, he would have known Mom would have instantly thrown that in the trash. She didn't, but she also didn't drink it. Her manners and good graces extended only as far as Tim Horton's coffee, at which she would turn her nose up and choose water instead.

Daryl is our family friend, a man with sarcasm as large as his huge compassion for others. A paramedic by training, he is calm, focused, and knowledgeable about everything. A realist by nature of profession, but one that feels deeply. He remembers everything, including all of our coffee orders. Janet, his wife, keeps him in line, and he'll be the first to admit that's no easy feat but one she does with joy. Daryl and Janet were the perfect balance for Mom and Dad. The four of them were often found laughing and swatting each other over terrible jokes.

When we arrived at the hospital, we had to check Dad in at the registration desk next to the decrepit emergency room, despite him being already admitted to the Cardiac Surgery Intensive Care Unit.

"Does John Doe G have any allergies?" the clerk asked without looking up from her keyboard.

"You mean Rod. Does Rod have any allergies?" Mom replied, annoyance evident in her voice that the clerk could not be bothered to use Dad's name, which we had given to her moments before.

"Does Rod have any allergies?" the clerk continued, nonplussed.

"No," Mom replied.

Quickly I interrupted. "Yes, he's allergic to codeine." I was now as annoyed as Mom that she couldn't remember what the love of her life was deathly allergic to. In hindsight, perhaps the stress of the situation made her forgetful. Lord knows there was just a little stress at that moment.

As soon as we registered Dad, Daryl led Mom and I up to the second floor to wait outside the cath lab. As we sat in chairs more uncomfortable than church pews, we realized that one member of our family was still in blissful ignorance.

Cody, who is two years younger than me, is as complex as he is wonderful. He loves people deeply, and family is important to him. In his time at Briercrest, more than a handful of our cousins were there at the same time, and he made efforts to connect with them all. On the volleyball court, he is competitive and inspiring. Values guide his decisions. His sarcasm and one-liners are the stuff of legend. He can make people laugh with a sideways glance, and two seconds later, give them the fiercest of hugs to let them know that they are loved.

Yet no matter how old Cody gets or mature he grows, he will always be my little brother. He likes to correct me that he's actually bigger than I am, but I'll stick with my characterization.

It was an unwritten rule in our house that we protected Cody. I was regularly told as a child that it was my job to look out for him, to take care of him. This was likely a function of being the oldest sibling rather than Cody actually needing it. Because, in fact, rarely did he need any protecting. I tried to help him with flashcards for science classes so he could excel. I was supposed to keep bullies away; I tried, almost got suspended, and ultimately failed. It was often my job to feed us dinner each night before our respective volleyball practices. Whether spoken or not, I felt responsible for being a proxy parent to Cody while Mom and Dad worked or got us to our games and practices. Unfortunately, in trying to protect him, we stunted him and likely belittled him.

So why not include him? It wasn't that Cody couldn't handle it. Despite our intense hovering, he did turn into an incredibly strong and brave man. We thought we knew better, but we certainly didn't. And to this day, we don't.

So in an effort to protect him, we rallied his troops just as we had when Mom was first diagnosed with cancer. We called the people he relied on and told them to be on standby because he would get some news that he would need help processing.

And then Mom called him.

This was the first of what would, unfortunately, be many bad news calls to Cody.

Later that night, when they moved Dad into the Cardiac Surgery Intensive Care Unit, we overheard some nurses talking as we waited outside.

"That John G patient is strong. Did you see him pulling on his restraints?" they muttered as they wandered past.

Mom, Adam, and I looked at each other. *What did they mean by restraints?* When we were finally allowed into the CSICU, all things were explained.

"Your husband," the doctor said to Mom, "is a very fit man. We've never had someone so fit in the CSICU. We tried to reduce his sedation, but as we did, he panicked and tried to pull out his breathing tube and catheter. We have to keep him sedated for his own safety. We also had to restrain him for the same reasons." The doctor's forehead wrinkled, frowning. He seemed struck by Dad's state yesterday and where he was today. The two things didn't compute.

I looked at Dad in his bed, tubes coming out of what seemed like every hole in his body. For a man sedated, he did not look peaceful. His brow was furrowed, his hands clenched, his legs taut, and his colour was off—somewhere between the pale of someone who has the flu and the lifeless colour you see in someone when they are scared out of their minds. Perhaps I was mirroring his pallor: I was terrified.

Then I noticed his hands were tied in soft restraints attached to each side of the bed. But he had pulled so much at them that he had bent the frame of the hospital bed. Samson still had his hair.

Strength looks so different in different people. In Dad, it was physical; he was bending beds and fighting intubation to survive and come back to us. In Mom and I, strength was holding the family together through food and getting done what needed to be done. Displays of strengths are usually easy to spot. We see them, we compliment them, and they become a thing of legend. Strength can be a façade, a way of coping and proving to the world that we have things under control. But behind it, unseen, can be so much brokenness.

To friends and family, I looked like I had it under control. Mom's cancer couldn't shake me in 2014, and neither could Dad's heart attack in 2015. Calm, confident. My schedule managed, my work prioritized, meals planned, and rehab questions prepared for the doctors. But what I felt was an uncontrollable panic that, if I paused even for a moment, would come out through tears, yelling, and insomnia. I was scared. I was scared to think too far into the future about the changes that were out of my control. I was scared to live in the present amid the medical jargon that I couldn't decipher. I was scared to remember the past because that felt so far away now. So what tense could I live in if the past, present, and future were all non-options? There is nothing. So I just lived tense.

And tense turned to tears with what the doctor told us next.

"Rod also suffered a stroke. We call it a hypoxic injury—his brain, starved for oxygen from being down for twelve minutes before the paramedics were able to get his heartbeat back, was traumatized. We aren't sure which came first, the heart attack or stroke, but we do know that it's a miracle he survived. Less than 11% of people survive this if both a heart attack and stroke happen outside of the hospital. He's lucky."

The doctor caught his breath and breathed out deeply. Long. His eyes full of compassion, he quietly began to speak. "But what you need to know is that he also has a brain bleed as a result of the stroke. So between those things, and being without oxygen for twelve minutes, it's very likely he will have cognitive impact. He will have significant memory loss and personality changes. The Rod you knew will not be the Rod we can hopefully bring out of this sedation."

My tears came, but they were not of sorrow. They were of anger. "You don't know my dad. You don't know what he can do. He will never change," I yelled at the nurse who was charting at the foot of Dad's bed.

"Sweetie, you can hope that, and you can pray that. But in my experience, I've never seen it happen," the nurse replied condescendingly.

As I stoked Dad's hand and kissed his cheek that afternoon, I prayed and pleaded to be right. I begged for healing, for miracles, for restoration. I prayed that the dad I'd always known, the one full of softness, empathy, and humour, would be the dad who woke up.

I bartered, telling God I'd never stop testifying to His goodness if Dad returned to his old self. I wept, asking God to make sure Dad knew who we were when he awoke. I pleaded with God, "Just wake him up."

What I got three days later when they reduced his sedation were a lot of half-answered prayers.

006: MOVING TO OKAY

Time went slowly in those first weeks. We fell into a predictable routine. Cody would come home for short weekend trips and longer ones between work commitments. Adam, in the middle of busy season as a public practice accountant, met us all at the hospital in the evenings. Or he'd take care of the things that needed to be done at home. The laundry that never ended. The housework that seemed to pile up even though we were never there. He did that for two households, even tackling Mom's early spring yard work while Dad was out of commission.

Food marked Dad's one-month stay at Royal Columbian Hospital. Each meal would come on a cold, beige tray with a covered plate and a teacup with a plastic lid. Chilled cutlery, creamer, and packs of sugar accompanied the lukewarm Red Rose. Next to these was a half sheet of paper listing the contents of the tray that was always read by Dad as, "One milker, one sugarar, one tea-er."

What started as a bit of a joke, wondering if Dad could actually read the menu, turned into a calming ritual for all who came to his room. He could, in fact, still read. Comprehension was another thing entirely. When his future felt so uncertain, we could be certain about this routine. This simple phrase reminded us that he was here, that the moment we were in was the only thing that was certain. After so much seriousness and so much worry, this was something predictable and something that turned relatively normal. We would hold on to this in the days and weeks that would come in the hospital.

We spent the first days of Dad's stay in the cardiac unit fighting for a private room for him. Mom was adamant that we would and should get Dad into his own room, no matter the cost. He deserved it. The love of her life deserved nothing but the best. He became more alert, and we realized that this was for his sanity as much as our own; the roommates in his shared room were even worse off than he was. Private rooms did come with a challenge, though; while the nursing staff were attentive, they were in the room for less time than if four people were sharing 200 square feet, all requiring attention. With Dad's natural stubbornness, he began to attempt to get out of bed at night without help. We returned one morning to a sign in his room that, in bold letters, tried to remind him: "PUSH THE RED BUTTON BEFORE YOU GET OUT OF BED."

Soon, though, Dad's persistence paid off. With support from the physiotherapist and Daryl, he slowly began taking steps down the hall and, eventually, up the stairs. His physical prowess hadn't left him yet. The hours he'd spent on his bike and in the gym were paying dividends now. Taking steps at this stage of recovery was astonishing. But to see him walk, hunched over and reliant on others, was equal parts joyful and pitiful. Here was a man who regularly cycled 150 kilometres in a day, now shuffling in his grey, grippy socks with his hospital gown open at the back, clutching the elbow of his best friend. How can two emotions like joy and pity coexist so easily?

I wish I had a rich, philosophical answer to that question. I wish I knew how and why we can experience such a dichotomy of emotions simultaneously, or how one situation can produce so many different feelings. In the absence of any firm answer, what I will offer is this: without knowing one, you can't know the other. Without knowing sorrow, you can't know joy. Without knowing peace, you can't know anger, and without knowing happiness, you can't know pity. The human condition is full of each of these; they are what make us beautiful and broken simultaneously. The spectrum of emotions is as diverse as people, and if we can strive to appreciate everyone for what they bring to the world, why can't we appreciate all these emotions for the same thing?

As Dad's physical health was gaining traction, thanks in part to his grippy, hospital-issued socks, his mental health was stalling. As his awareness and ability to communicate grew, we realized how much damage the stroke had done to his brain.

It was most evident in his short-term memory. Left alone, Dad was terrified. Whether it was the beeping of IV machines every few minutes, the restless neighbours next door in the ward, or his ever-growing awareness that he should remember something but he couldn't, he struggled with being alone. So he regularly asked for his cell phone. He wanted to have it in his pocket or beside his bed so he could hold it, touch it, and have something familiar close by. He wanted to know that he could press one button and voices he recognized would be on the other end. Imagine questioning the surety that is your own brain. Not being able to trust that you know where you are, that you know who you are. Imagine questioning every moment whether you are safe. Imagine being so frustrated in your inability to remember that you want to punch your fist through a wall because maybe, just maybe, you will remember what pain feels like. At least that would be something familiar.

Mom decided that it wasn't a good idea for Dad to have his phone while he was in the hospital. She worried he would lose it and make his anxiety worse. But every night he would cry out, looking for his phone. He would push the red call button, asking the nurses for his phone. Finally, Mom wrote a note in her handwriting and taped it up on his wall, next to the sign from the nurses.

EMILY HAS YOUR CELL PHONE.

It is amazing what we come to rely on and fixate on when we can't trust ourselves. Dad was scared to be without his cell phone because he couldn't remember where he was, why he was there, or where his family was. He couldn't trust the one thing that had never failed him: his brain. So his lifeline became his mobile line. His ability to connect with his family was what would keep him sane and keep him from getting out of bed. If he couldn't trust himself, he needed to be able to trust those around him.

While we noticed most of Dad's memory loss in his inability to recollect family stories or the day's events, the doctors were acutely aware of his declining executive functioning capabilities. His ability to make decisions, manage time, plan ahead, or control himself was significantly reduced. His working memory was virtually non-existent. It could have been a result of the stroke, or maybe the brain bleed that accompanied it. Perhaps it was a concussion from when he fell off the bike. The on-call neurologist conducted two different tests to accurately determine the strength of Dad's cognitive abilities. One he called the letter mail test. He asked this simple question: "Rod, if you saw a stamped, sealed, and addressed envelope on the sidewalk, what would you do with it?"

To most, the answer is obvious: drop it in a mailbox.

But Dad's response was far from obvious. "Hmmmmm. I'd try to walk it to the address on it."

The doctor countered, "What if that address was in Ontario?"

"Or maybe I'd bring it to the house close by. I'd open it. I don't know what I would do." Exasperated by not knowing the right answer, Dad looked away. Shutting down.

The doctor's next test involved what is called a Montreal Cognitive Assessment, or MoCA for short. The MoCA is designed to test for mild cognitive impairment by doing a series of activities and scoring the participant out of thirty points. It involves things like drawing a clock face, naming animals, remembering words, identifying letters, and finding similarities between two things. For most adults, a score of 26 or 27 is normal. A score of 18–25 indicates mild cognitive impairment, while a score of 11–21 is where most Alzheimer's patients fall.

Dad scored a 7.

Objective scores, rankings, and data have always been my preference. There is a clear definition of success, and a clear winner and loser. In this case, we were not winners. We weren't even close to winning.

"Rayel," the doctor began, "you need to understand that this is a very low score."

Tell me something that I don't know.

He continued, "This is likely the result of the brain bleed, the stroke, and a concussion from when he fell from his bike. With occupational therapy, we could see that score increase by a few points, but it is very unlikely that it will rise to a normal level again. The injury was in a part of the brain that controls decision-making and initiation. Sometimes, even personality."

"How can I help him? What can we do?" I queried.

"Right now, you need to give him time to heal, and he needs to get into rehab for some occupational therapy. I'd recommend Queen's Park or Laurel Place. I'll put in a referral now, but it may take some time."

Time was something that I didn't feel we had. If Dad was going to return to normal, it needed to be now. It needed to happen soon, while his personality was still close to the surface, or maybe he would be gone forever. Worried he would change permanently if things didn't get better, I escalated the urgency on every decision, every action. That Dad that I clung so tightly to, the one who could make me laugh with an eyebrow raise, needed to stay close. My own sanity depended on it.

Daryl was a strong advocate for Dad to move to Laurel Place rather than Queen's Park, believing the quality of care would be better at Laurel Place, an extension of Surrey Memorial Hospital. His opinion always carried weight with Mom. She considered him more of an expert in medical things than some of the doctors we came across. So she too began to advocate for a Laurel Place move. And not only that, but she would not let the hospital discharge Dad until there was a spot at the rehab unit ready for him. With her work schedule, she could not care for him at home.

Deep down, she knew that if she brought him home, getting him back to the hospital would be a monumental challenge. His anxiety over leaving the house and being "committed" again would not go well. This meant that Dad would stay in an overflow hospital unit for almost two weeks while we waited for a bed. In this unit, we saw fifteen patients separated by curtains with no room for chairs beside their beds, crammed into a room that was the size of a suburban living room. The room was loud and so full that you could feel the sweat from the patient in the next bed. Mom and I refused to spend time there, so each time we would visit, we would take Dad for a walk: Starbucks, Brown's, the cafeteria. We all needed better food than what we could find at the hospital. Food sustained us, both physically and emotionally, as it always had.

Food is one of those things that my memories centre around, not just for these particular moments. As a kid, I remember family Christmases not because of what presents I received but because of what we ate. Grandma Quiring's buns reminded me of her kisses and unconditional love. Grandma Isaak's sweets felt like a hug, wrapping me up and spoiling me rotten. Dad's Christmas dinners sparked endless conversations on flavour, roasting techniques, and whether the stuffing was too sagey for our liking. Mom's small-portion, elegant dinners intertwine in my memory with conversation as rich as the food we were eating. Food has the ability to not only draw out memories but also to impact our emotions.

One morning in early March 2015, we got the call that a bed had opened up at Laurel Place. Dad would be on a transport that afternoon. Daryl had been ever-present at the hospital, whenever he wasn't attending to patients in his ambulance, and was excited to come with us to the rehab unit. Our goodbye to Royal Columbian was anticlimactic; we were all ready for a new chapter and to be one step closer to home, both physically and metaphorically. Dad was nervous in the transport, strapped to a wheelchair. His hands, clasped together, were white-knuckled, with the exception of his thumbs, which were tapping his hands rhythmically. This had become his telltale anxious tic since his stroke.

As we entered the rehab unit, we both looked around nervously until Daryl reappeared. He smiled, he laughed, and he strode confidently in front of us, leading us to the fourth floor and the locked-down unit. He showed us around, introduced us to the unit clerk, and we found Dad his room. It was large, roughly double the size of his private hospital room, with a single bed, a private bathroom, and a window that opened. In healthcare terms, it was luxury. Clearly feeling at home, Dad quickly made himself comfortable on the bed, turning on the TV and lying down with his one hand behind his head. True to form, Daryl jumped into the tiny bed with him, and as the two almost-brothers lay side-by-side, we knew everything was going to be okay.

Or, at least, we prayed it would.

* * *

In Dad's nondescript room at Laurel Place, there was a whiteboard that listed all of his therapists and his release date. Upon admission to the unit, he looked at the board and stated, "I have an occupational the rapist, a physio the rapist, and a speech the rapist."

I gasped, eyes darting in every direction to make sure no one heard him. "Dad! It's therapist. You have these therapists."

He slowly broke into that cheeky smile of his, where his eyes gleam with mischievousness and his shoulders start quaking before his chuckle even comes out. "But it says THE rapist!"

I will never look at the word therapist again without groaning at the dad joke that kept us laughing on move-in day.

On that move-in day, the unit clerk put a note on Dad's whiteboard that he would be released two weeks later, March 23. Dad saw that and was immediately ecstatic; he would be out in time for his birthday and in time for some real food! Mom and I thought that it was best to manage his expectations, and we quickly erased any date at all. At this point, controlling access to information for others was something we just did without thinking. It was as normal to her and I as breathing. In some cases, it was needed, and in others, a gross overstep of others' rights. A habit that, to this day, I regularly need to check myself on.

Two weeks turned into three months. Arduous doesn't begin to describe that time for any of us while Dad was in cardiac rehab. For Dad, he passed the physiotherapy requirements in his first week, thanks in part to his incredible fitness before his stroke and his inherent stubbornness. So the remaining eleven weeks were focused on occupational therapy. Pam, his wonderful, patient, and incredibly persistent occupational therapist, kept him focused and progressing. But after a stroke in the area of the brain his was in, progress was measured differently.

No longer could Dad solve complex structural engineering problems, convert units of measure, or even figure out how to mail a letter that was stamped. Things that come as second nature to adults became unattainable goals for him.

Still, Dad regularly went looking for his cell phone. Because of his memory impairment, Mom had yet to return it after confiscating it and taking it home for safekeeping, but he panicked daily, looking for it. He had a landline in his room and would call me each day at work using my phone number that he'd written in the front of his daily schedule notebook.

"Rayel," he'd begin in tears, "I can't find my cell phone."

"Hi, Dad. Mom has your cell phone at home. You don't have it with you," I'd reply calmly.

"Oh, okay. Thanks then. Bye." He'd hang up quickly.

Then this same call would happen, verbatim, another thirty-seven times in the next forty-five minutes. I always picked up. Perhaps this was why he continued to call me first. He must have trusted that I would be on the other end. The calls only ended because of meal times or occupational therapy sessions. I've never been an overly patient person; I would regularly roll my eyes at Starbucks when my ridiculously complicated London Fog took more than two minutes for the barista to make. But this, I had all the patience in the world for. This stream of phone calls continued for weeks, abating as his executive functioning somewhat returned. It didn't matter to me. My patience never wavered.

I'd like to pretend that I matured in that time and developed this incredible patience that has never left me, but that would be a lie. The only reason I was able to stay calm and keep my eyes from rolling at Dad each day was because of God. Somehow, I got God's patience and made it through repetitive conversations and questions with ease. The grace I had for Dad was limitless; I knew that this wasn't what he wanted and wasn't who he was. It was a supernatural gift, a grace bestowed on me by a God who knew exactly what we needed to get through this season. Those are my favourite gifts from God, ones that make no sense to me yet meet my needs so precisely that there is no explanation other than them being from a loving Father who knows me better than I know myself.

007: LOVE TRUMPS ALL

It was a Thursday night in April, which meant that Adam would be leading youth at church for several hours. He claimed it was to mentor middle school boys. Still, every Thursday he would come home with new stories about dumb things they did and moments that only thirteen-year-olds would find hilarious. For him, it was about having fun and influencing the lives of boys who needed a strong role model. I believe that in the back of his mind, it was also about having a break from the realities of being an accountant and a husband, all the while dealing with his sick in-laws. Every Thursday since Dad's heart attack, I'd spend that husband-less, father-less Thursday evening taking a long, hot shower and watching an anxiety-reducing show like *Friends* on Netflix before succumbing to sleep at an hour my grandmother would be proud of. This Thursday was no different.

Until Adam woke me up when he got home. Usually I would wake up with a start when he would get home because the sound of his keys jingling somehow interrupted whatever part of the REM cycle I was in. But this Thursday, I woke up to a gentle touch and a soft, "Babe, wake up."

"What's going on? What time is it?" I asked in a fog. It was 10:30 p.m.

"I got a call from Daryl. Your mom called him and Janet. Something's wrong. She's being flown home from Edmonton, and they're bringing her to the hospital."

My brain woke up, recalling facts instantly. She was in Edmonton on business. Due back tomorrow. Supposed to make sure Dad got clean clothes. The combination of to-dos and facts intertwined.

Tears immediately sprang to my eyes, and I sat up in my morning-ready gym clothes. "Where are they taking her?"

"Abbotsford. They want us to meet her there."

It took a quick text to my co-coach, a brush of the teeth, and a grab of my phone charger before we ran to the truck. Every part of my body tensed as we raced to meet Mom in the one place I did not want to go back to: the Cancer Centre. The entire drive there, I tried to both piece together what might have happened and to start remembering what protocol she had a year earlier when cancer first made its appearance.

We beat them to the hospital, and we waited. As soon as Daryl pulled up, he grabbed a wheelchair for Mom and brought her inside. She looked both determined and confused. Her eyes were sharp, but she was looking around her to take in clues about what had happened. We hugged as we waited in triage, but thanks to her handy, red "I have cancer" card, we saw a nurse immediately and rushed inside. In typical Mom fashion, she hadn't mentioned to me that she had a lump, about the size of a shot glass, growing on the top of her head. It hid like a snake under her thick, regrown hair, waiting to pounce. In her mind, she chalked it up to an irregular mole. Maybe I should have questioned her mental state at that point. In retrospect, she was falling into her habit of controlling the situation—if I didn't know about the lump, I couldn't worry. Ignorance, for both of us, would be bliss.

After checking in, Daryl gave us the rundown. This time, this relapse, Mom had been on a business trip, inspecting one of her sites in Edmonton. While there, all of a sudden she wasn't making any sense. When asked what the colour of the floor was, her reply was "Horse." Her regular headache worsened, and she lost sight in her left eye. At least, this is what the colleague who was with her in Edmonton told Daryl when their WestJet flight touched down.

Adam, Mom, and I spent the night in emergency, until Mom sent us home at 4:00 a.m. There was nothing we could do until the oncologist reviewed the scans, and she wouldn't be in until the workday started. Sleeping upright in her chair, Mom sent us to my in-laws' house for some rest and hot coffee. Sleep eluded me, with my mind wandering through worst-case scenarios and the logistics of now having two parents in two separate hospitals.

Two parents, two different hospitals, two terrible diseases. What was this life? I was twenty-six years old, six months married, and I was supposed to be living a vastly different story. We were dreaming of big trips, career opportunities, and building our network of friends together. Adam and I expected to have our biggest stressor be how to choose between breweries on a Friday night. We had plans to be living large and carefree in that fun stage before kids made an appearance.

And as empty nesters with privilege and means, my parents had a different plan for themselves too. Trips to white sand beaches, or wine nights with friends. Their next season was to hold more work than play. More time volunteering or building a relationship with their kids as adults.

Instead, I was sitting up at 4:00 a.m., wondering how I was going to tell my brother that our mom's cancer had relapsed. I was crying, thinking about how many times I would have to explain to my memory-impaired father that his wife of thirty years was sitting in another hospital, in another city, and would require brain surgery. I was constantly checking our bank statements to make sure that we could afford to have me take unpaid time off to be with my family and still afford the coffee that everyone around me desperately needed.

Adam reassured me all he could and kept us afloat financially and otherwise. People offered and asked what they could do, but I had no idea what they could do . . . I didn't even know what to do! I couldn't delegate what I didn't know.

I was wondering how to balance my time between two sick parents who both deserved every ounce of my love and attention, as did my brand-new husband, who did everything in his power to allow me to be with them. With all that in mind, at twenty-six and six months married, I gave my husband an out. "Babe, I love you, and I love being your wife, but this is not what you signed up for. This isn't going away. If you want to go or even take a break, I'll get it. This is more than we bargained for, and this isn't fair to you. I'm so sorry."

"Rayel. Stop; don't ever say that again. I love you, and I married you, and I'm here. I'm not going anywhere. They are my family too, and I am here for you every step of the way."

"Adam, I'm so sorry."

"Stop it. You have nothing to apologize for. Now go back to sleep."

This conversation repeated itself for a few nights before I realized that he really didn't want to go anywhere, that he wouldn't go anywhere. This was a fear that continued to ravage my brain for months and years to come. *Why would anyone want to be with a broken woman who doesn't have time or emotional space for them? Or choose to stay in a situation where their partner lives on wine and coffee, waiting for a tense phone call? How could he want to put up with more sobbing than words coming out of my mouth?* I needed him, even if I couldn't articulate it. And I couldn't possibly lose one more thing, one more person.

That is love. It's not easy, and it isn't supposed to be. It's sacrifice, it's work, and it's a challenge to remain committed. And love is worth the hardship. Love makes it possible to walk through anything. That's the beauty of love. There's no questioning integrity or motives; it's simply that the other person matters more than you. It's about laying down your dreams, your desires, for the other person. Your priority is no longer yourself. Your selfish ambition is no longer the driving force. It's about someone else. It's unconditional. It's freeing. And that is exactly the love that Adam showed me both then and every day since.

And then I had to call Cody. It was 7:00 a.m. the morning after Mom was first brought into triage at the hospital. I'd had more coffees than hours of sleep by that point, and my brain was remarkably sharp for one that generally requires ten or more hours of sleep.

"Cody," I began. "Something happened." I think it's possible to hear someone's shoulders rise and their heart start to race over the phone because that's precisely what I heard. I continued.

"It's Mom. She was in Edmonton yesterday and she started getting confused, so they put her on a plane home. She's at the hospital now. It looks like her cancer is spreading to her brain."

"Dang. Not again," he said quietly as he began to cry.

I find it awkward when other people grieve over something that I am supposed to grieve over. It's like I don't know what to do. Should I say something, do something, or pretend to cry alongside them? I truly believe that the ability to grieve in groups is a gift not everyone has. I certainly don't. Cody was in shock, crying softly into the phone, and while I wanted to mirror his emotions, I couldn't. The awkward part of me came out, and I remained emotionless, pragmatic. I focused on the clinical explanation of Mom's situation rather than the human one. It felt sociopathic being so detached from her human experience; it probably looked like I didn't care, or that it didn't bother me. The truth of the matter is, it bothered me very much. I just did not have the skills to deal with it alongside other people. I instantly regretted how I came across, but my emotional intelligence failed me and I could not be like a chameleon and get my emotions to match the situation.

Cody began asking questions about what was happening, and I started making up the answers, piecing together the bits of information I knew. To tell a story that made sense. I'd read enough WebMD articles and had enough conversations with nurses at that point to feel like an expert. So I pretended to be one, giving him positive answers and hope where it might not exist, to protect him. And, I think, to protect me.

It is obvious that I wanted to protect him from hurt, but less apparent was the guilt I tried to save him from. When he made the decision years before to move to the prairies, I knew that would mean that although he would be there for the big milestones, it would also mean that he would be missing out on the everyday moments. And for a kid who had a strong sentimental side, I thought this would prove incredibly challenging. As I sat on Bonnie's well-worn blue futon, I knew I couldn't give him the full truth about the seriousness of what Mom was about to face. All in a misguided effort to protect him. I wanted him to know that his choice to be apart was okay, that it was not laden with expectations. I wanted him to know that this was handled, that his absence was felt, but not so much that we couldn't do it without him. He wasn't slacking in his duties as a son or brother. There was nothing we could do.

In writing this story, I grew to learn that my actions actually did the opposite of my intention. Cody felt guilty anyway. I learned that he felt isolated. His trust in me eroded because he knew the whole story wasn't coming through. He wanted to be involved, to help, and to do as much as he possibly could, and I simply wasn't giving him the opportunity.

I wasn't allowing him to feel in control of anything because I needed that control myself. When things happen to us that we don't expect, it's easy to feel the need to control the things we can so we don't have the feeling that we've lost all control. Sometimes it's so that we have a reason for the outcome—that we didn't do enough, or we did the wrong thing, or that we didn't have enough faith. I took control so I could rationalize what was happening to our family and left Cody to ride the waves of guilt and grief in his own boat. It's an action that I am deeply sorry about to this day.

Eventually, we found out that the breast cancer we'd thought was gone for good had returned and metastasized in Mom's brain. It was this new tumour that was causing her eyesight to be so poor and her words to be jumbled. Her neurosurgeon was a confident man who explained the impending brain surgery so quickly and in so much jargon that neither of us had any questions, simply because we didn't know what we could challenge him on. And for two smart women, that was very, very unusual. Mom spent the next few days at home, and we were able to spend more time with Dad while we waited for her surgery date.

A few days later, Mom went to Royal Columbian in New Westminster for surgery by transport ambulance. We perched outside the operating room in the same chairs that we'd sat in while Dad was undergoing his heart surgery just a few months before. I reflected on that day in a social media post:

> In this chair, I have experienced the most agonizing sorrow I can imagine. I have heard some of the hardest words and dreamed the worst dreams. In this chair, I have cried to the point that it hurt every bone in my body. In this chair, I thought everything was over.

> And in this chair, I found renewed hope and joy. In this chair, I have found my faith to grow and my family healed. In this chair, I cried tears of joy and smiled for the first time in weeks. In this chair, I learned that you never really have to sit by yourself. While things aren't perfect, God commanded us to move forward with courage and strength. Today,

Mom & Dad, I do that for you. Because love hopes
all things, bears all things, and endures all things.

After two hours of butt-numbing time in that chair, Adam and I
caught a glimpse of the surgeon walking with some nurses down an
adjacent, staff-only hallway. Immediately we stood up, heart racing
and eyes ready to burst with tears as I asked him, "How's my mom?"

His response was oddly nonchalant. "She's fine. It's just
brain surgery."

My jaw hit the floor. Adam was amused. How could a surgeon be
so non-emotional about what we were going through? Did he not
realize that we had been dreading this for days, and that we arrived
here in an ambulance? Did he not recall every TV drama depicting
that brain surgery was the most serious thing in the world and that
almost every character had some sort of near-death experience while
on the operating table?

When finally allowed into the recovery room, I saw Mom curled
up under her warm blanket, hair intact, and smiling a lazy half smile.
I finally believed the neurosurgeon. I was expecting breathing tubes
and a bald patch on her head. Instead, I got the perfect picture of
someone at peace. Sure, she was medicated, but she was relaxed and
happy. Relieved, I asked if we could record a video to show to Dad
and relieve his anxiety about her surgery. We turned on my phone's
camera, and she smiled as she said, "Dear Rodney, how are you? I've
had some good surgery. I have some staples back here, not very many.
Little bit of a headache, but I will see you soon. Love you, have a
great night."

It was the perfect love letter to the man who cared so deeply for
her that his own brain trauma could not take away his worry about
her brain surgery. A man who could forget where he placed a pencil
ten seconds earlier but could not forget the pain his wife was walking
through. It was an offering of peace to a man who, earlier that day,

had desperately tried to use his electric shaver as a phone to call the woman he loved, to make sure she was safe.

When we love deep enough, like Dad loved Mom, we don't feel the weight of our own problems. We are able to ignore our aches and pains, and even sometimes our trauma, for the sake of someone else. This self-sacrificing love is exactly how Jesus loved us, and it is our example to follow. We love because He first loved us, and loved us in a way that doesn't make sense and that seems extraordinary. But isn't that what all love is? Extraordinary. And it is so worth it.

008: SURRENDERING THE FIGHT

A few weeks after the brain surgery, I hosted a baby shower for a close friend, and Mom attended. As soon as she walked in, in her new yellow jeans, I knew something was the matter. Her knee had been sore for a few weeks, causing her to limp and prompting late night runs to the pharmacy for Voltaren and a brace.

That day, it seemed worse than ever before. Walking into the amenities room in our complex, taking the lone step to get into the building, she felt something crack. Surprisingly, she actually admitted it to me, and that's when I knew this was no ordinary event.

With her typical grace and class, she acted as though nothing was bothering her. She played queen, sitting regally in her chair, waving across the room and regaling those who sat next to her with stories. But she never got up, never refilled the coffee I'd brought her. That was the odd part: that she wouldn't get up. No matter what, Mom had always circulated the room—maybe to make her presence known or to ensure those around her felt loved. I'll never really know. Likely it was both.

When I was in university, Mom brought me to a networking event put on by the Vancouver Board of Trade at the Pan Pacific Hotel. The room was full of city bigwigs, and Mom felt like she belonged there. In fact, she did belong there. By role title and by affiliation. It was a lunch meeting, with some presenter speaking on a topic that went in one ear and out the other. But what I do remember is that I saw the president of the Vancouver Board of Trade, and Mom made sure that I went and introduced myself to him. She showed me how to scope the room for an opening and introduction to tell him that I was a member of the Leaders of Tomorrow program.

One thing Mom always instilled in Cody and I was that we could talk to people that were above us, whether in age or in status. She made sure that, even as kids, we knew how to carry a conversation while smiling and asking the right questions to make the other person feel heard and respected. She didn't come with me to meet the CEO, but she was watching from a distance, making sure that I felt supported, and probably watching to provide coaching notes after on how I could improve.

So for a woman who often would run the room or make sure that I did, it was weird to see her sitting in a chair, moving with her eyes instead of her feet. At the end of the day, when everyone had left the room, she asked me to bring her car around. I went and pulled her BMW up to the door and suddenly realized that Mom physically couldn't get out of the chair. I carried my mother in my arms, like I would eventually carry my son, the fifteen feet to her car. The next realization I had was that she couldn't drive her vehicle, so I jumped in to take her home.

When we got to the house, I looked at her and very quietly said, "Mom, I don't think this is right." We called Daryl, and with sadness in his voice, he told us that we needed to call for an ambulance. In fact, he did the calling for us to make sure the paramedics that came for us were top-notch and understood the severity of the situation.

In the dining room, I slowly undressed Mom out of those yellow jeans and into her sweatpants and comfortable shirt, because we both sensed this would be a long hospital stay. It was surreal to be the one that was getting her changed, knowing that this was the start of the end.

A few minutes later, the ambulance showed up unceremoniously with no lights, no sirens, and with very little speed. Daryl and Adam moved furniture out of the way so the paramedics could bring in the stretcher. They loaded Mom into the ambulance, and I jumped in beside her. In typical Mom fashion, she was jovial and trying to make light of a very difficult situation. Like always, she told the paramedics that it was arthritis and that it was just acting up because of the change in weather. As the paramedic and I made eye contact across Mom's stretcher, we both knew she was lying. I'll never know if she was lying to protect me, or if she just couldn't face the truth of it herself. I suspect it was both. The cancer was growing and taking over parts of her body that she had never anticipated.

As usual, we went to the emergency room and were quickly admitted because of that little red card that said she was an active cancer patient. That card brought us a lot of benefits, including never having to be in the waiting room in a hospital. But it was also a stark reminder that something wasn't right. The seriousness of the situation matched the boldness of the red on the card.

After being admitted to the oncology ward yet again, things started to feel different. At first, the oncologist thought that this was cartilage cancer and sent Mom to Vancouver General Hospital for a scan. Within days of receiving the scan, it became clear that this wasn't a new type of cancer. This was breast cancer, now metastasized in her bones. It was then that we knew this wasn't going away, and that any success we'd had and getting clean margins during the brain tumour removal didn't matter. This disease was quickly taking over her body. First her breast, then her brain, and now her bones.

I remember the doctor coming into her room in Abbotsford to talk about the options for Mom. It wasn't the oncologist this time but a regular orthopedic surgeon. Immediately upon introducing himself, he launched right into his diagnosis, leaving no space for pleasantries or feelings. This man was clearly busy. His tone was clipped, and his words were belittling. His bedside manner left more than something to be desired, and both Mom and I got on the offensive very quickly.

He quickly told us that there was no feasible option and that surgery would not be able to get Mom walking again. "If we fix one leg," he declared, "then we will just have to fix the other at some point, and it's not like it will help a cancer this aggressive."

He offered no solutions, no recovery time. He spoke with authority, in statements rather than questions. There was no back and forth, simply directives by him as to what would happen. Namely, nothing.

Finally, with complete exasperation and anger, I rudely asked, "Well, what the hell is the other option to make her walk?"

Equally as rudely, he looked at me and responded tritely, "You need to understand that she will never walk again."

At that moment, the world seemed to crash around me. It was like every hope I had held on to that this would be fixable, like the brain tumour, was false. It was like someone telling me that there was no need to fight anymore. We were being told to give up.

I've only ever tried to give up once in my life. Well, that's probably a hyperbole, but one that I distinctly remember. It was piano lessons. Mom had put me in piano lessons to help me become more "cultured," which was her same rationale for putting me in ballet class. But unlike ballet, which I spent the better part of nine years attempting (and failing) to do gracefully, I just never took to piano. I couldn't handle sitting on my own and practising, and honestly, never getting better. Though, to be fair, the reason I never got better was because I never practised. It was an eight-year-old's catch-22. I viewed the actual piano lessons that my parents paid for as my practice time. So time and time again, I tried to quit piano lessons. I wasn't getting any better, so why keep going? But my parents sat me down at the piano and stayed with me for the thirty minutes that I needed to practice. Despite my repeated pleas to give up the instrument, they never let me. Ten years of piano lessons, and I can still barely remember the C scale. In fact, I remember Dad telling me that Quirings never quit in the middle of something. This phrase has stuck with me through many times when I've tried to throw my hands up and walk away—volleyball games, hard university classes, difficult work projects—but I know it's not in our DNA.

So being told by a doctor to give up and realize the gravity of the situation was not something I was prepared to do. This was something that we couldn't talk our way out of, problem solve our way out of, or pay our way out of. All we had left was prayer.

After he laid that bomb on us, I started sobbing and shaking uncontrollably. Maybe it was that he had said the truth out loud that Mom had been afraid to face, or maybe it was that she knew she had to be strong for me, but Mom instantly had peace and clarity. She thanked the doctor. He turned quickly and bolted, almost as if he didn't want to see the tears he knew were coming. Mom held on to me, stroking my hand softly, telling me that it would be okay. I told her that we would find a way out of this, that we would find another doctor. She looked me squarely in the face, deep in my eyes, and told me that we weren't going to find another doctor.

"How could you just give up?" I asked in between sobs and wiping snot from my nose.

She didn't answer my question. Instead, she replied, "Rayel, I love you. I am so proud of you, and you will always be my daughter."

These words. These words are what have dragged me through the last seven years of ups and downs. The words that I've come back to every time that I can't see straight. Which feels almost daily. When the moments of motherhood overtake me, and when the reality of missing my mom hits deep, these words replay in my mind. These have turned into the words that I repeat to my own children, words that I hope give them the strength that they have given me.

Mom held me, putting one hand on my shoulder, and the other stroking my hair. I could smell her vitamin E lotion, and I felt her hand work its way through the knots in my hair, just like it had when I was a child. Her heart beat firmly, steadily. Reminding me that she was still here and that no matter what, her heart was beating for me. Time seemed to stop as I sat there smelling her, feeling her, and soaking in every second of that precious time.

Eventually the nurse came in with warm blankets for us both, and more tissues for me. Mom sat up as best she could and pretended like nothing had happened. Her regular go-to move—diffusing the situation of emotions. It was on to something else. I asked if I could spend the night, willing to sleep in the most uncomfortable blue fold-up chair.

"Rayel, I'm fine. Go home," she said.

"No, Mom. I'm staying."

And she let me. We read Psalms together. In hindsight, I don't really know if Mom and I ever read the Bible out loud together, other than a few daily devotionals when I was a child. And it felt forced now that we both understood that the end was near. It was like we were forcing memories to happen, the ones that you want to take pictures of, to be able to say, later on, that you did. But we did it. With the idea that she would be confined to a hospital bed for the rest of her life, barring a miracle, we both intuited the same. This was another step toward the end.

I remember that I was falling asleep in that room, listening to Mom breathe deep breaths. She was never a quiet sleeper, despite her trying to blame her snores on Dad, especially when we camped in the trailer. But listening to her sleep somewhat peacefully gave me the sense that she had accepted what the doctors had said and that she knew. She knew what was going to happen to her. And there was no fear in that. No sense of anxiety about where she'd end up, even a moment of clarity. I'm not sure if this is something that every dying person gets or at what point the peace that surpasses understanding really sets in. But I know that it hit her that night. I know she was ready to meet Jesus, and that she was ready to leave us. But I knew I wasn't ready to let her go.

009: IT TAKES A VILLAGE

It was while Dad was in rehab at Laurel Place, part of Surrey Memorial Hospital, that Mom entered Abbotsford Regional Hospital with her brain tumour. Two parents, two different hospitals, forty minutes apart. Suddenly, my three-job, flexible coaching situation became the most enabling thing in my life. My days fell into a predictable routine. I would leave my house at 5:17 a.m. for work, and not a moment sooner. At 11:30 a.m., I'd call it quits and drive from Richmond to Surrey to spend time with Dad. We'd chat, go to his occupational therapy session, and then walk across the street to Starbucks. After our oat fudge bars and the strongest coffee they make, I'd drop Dad off back in his room and head to Abbotsford.

The afternoons I spent with Mom. We discussed my parents' finances, where important documents were located, and the litany of paperwork that needed to get done for their extended health insurers. It felt like an afternoon of business meetings, though my COO was wearing a hospital gown and toque to cover her bald head. Her nails, though—those were on point, manicured, gelled, and pristine. Then I'd head home, exhausted. Dinners with Adam were generally take-out in front of the TV. We'd give each other the rundown on the day, though sometimes we'd cross paths on the highway, him headed to see Dad in Surrey and me headed to Abbotsford to see Mom. We'd chat about our days, and I'd give him instructions on what he needed to do with Dad or check in on. Regardless of the afternoon and early evening activities, around 8:00 p.m. he would go back to his computer to tackle another day of busy season, and I'd go to bed an hour later. The nights were long. The nightmares were real. The insomnia was occasional. One night, after tossing and turning for several hours, I got up and made eggs benedict at 3:00 a.m. Hollandaise sauce goes great with *Grey's Anatomy*.

Why is it that we fixate on the most random objects during times of stress and grief? I can remember the shade and length of Mom's nails, but I couldn't tell you which file her RRSP documents were located in, despite her telling me no less than six times. I can remember the way she texted with those nails, typing in a super awkward way to avoid the clackety-clack sound. Yet those key discussions about wills and executors are barely a memory at all. When my brain wanted to shut down and shut off from the stress of it all, my body focused on the physical things it could see, hear, and smell. The certainty that the physical world provided offered a semblance of normal in a situation that was anything but.

With Dad calling an extraordinary number of times each day to question where his cell phone was, I was nervous to tell him about Mom's reappearing cancer. The absolute last thing I wanted to do each day was break his heart.

Can you imagine the pain he could have been in? Every time you attempt to call your wife, you can't get in touch with her. So you call your daughter and ask about her. And then you are told she has cancer and is in the hospital again. Your deepest love and best friend is in the hospital and there is absolutely nothing you can do about it; you can't see her or support her. You are trapped by your mind and rehab unit, with their doubly locked doors. Your heart hurts, your breathing labours, and your tears come fast and furious. Your shoulders tense, and your brain goes through every worst-case scenario. The woman you've spent your entire life knowing and loving is alone and dying. And you go through this heart-wrenching process each time you pick up the phone, which is almost every other minute that you are awake.

But God, in his ever-loving wisdom, gave us so much grace. Mom's diagnosis would be the sole thing that Dad could remember. He didn't ask what was wrong with her; he knew. He knew she had cancer, and he knew she was in the hospital. His heart was steadily breaking instead of freshly cracking in two each hour of the day. It doesn't seem like much of a relief for him, but it was.

This routine of mine continued for a few months, with a brief break when Mom was at her home in between her brain surgery and bone cancer discovery. Dad, however, stayed in rehab, getting only marginally better each day and becoming increasingly more frustrated that his release date was being pushed back. Finally, we had it set for June 1, and he could not have been more excited. He was like a kid waiting for Christmas; countdowns were happening, and he told everyone that he was going home.

Until he wasn't.

When Mom went back to the hospital after the bridal shower, I finally came to the conclusion that I couldn't do this alone anymore. Adam was supportive in every conceivable way, and friends were visiting my parents and bringing meals as often as they possibly could. But I never asked for help. I didn't want to ask for anything.

Growing up, asking for help was a sign of weakness, and doing so would show the world that we didn't have it all together. The façade of perfection would come crashing down, and that was something to be avoided at all costs. In some ways, this benefited Cody and I. We learned how to be self-sufficient and how to problem solve. We learned things that kids don't learn until they are adults. That bank accounts can draw into negative balances, that a ten-year-old making dinner for the family without using the stove requires extraordinary creativity, and that remembering all the gear you need for baseball games is your own responsibility.

These were not bad lessons to learn, but the darker side of over-indexed self-sufficiency is burnout. My parents, trying to hold it all together by themselves, regularly burned out. In the 90s, they wouldn't have called it that, but looking back, that's the label it deserves. I saw them asleep by 8:00 p.m. each night, easily irritated, and avoiding other people, always blaming it on busy schedules. This was generational; my grandparents were similar. As first-generation Canadians and Mennonite farmers on the prairies, self-sufficiency was a measure of success; the unending refrain of "you can do any-thing if you work hard enough" echoed throughout our farms and our homes. The irony of it all is that the more we had, the more we wanted to help those around us. We expected ourselves to. We couldn't ask for help, but we sure could give it. And if offered, we were to decline mildly so as not to burden others. If offered twice, the methodology told us we could accept. And we did. Sometimes.

So when I stared down the barrel of a mother fighting cancer in the hospital, and a brain-injured father returning home to an empty house, I lost it. I collapsed on the dirty carpet in my walkthrough closet and couldn't move. I was alone in the house. The absence of the hospital monitor beeping was almost overwhelming. Paralysis hit my limbs, and my eyes couldn't focus. Surprisingly, tears wouldn't come. My mental overwhelm was finally taking hold of my body. I couldn't do it anymore.

I couldn't fathom another day of answering Dad's same questions over and over again. The idea of moving back in to my parents' house to care for him made me physically nauseous. The deliberations of adding more responsibility to my already overfull plate made me crumple. But what was I supposed to do? These were my parents. They were struggling, and I could do it. I had to do it. I couldn't not. Love required it.

And if love required this sacrifice, shouldn't I be happy to do it? Shouldn't it be easy? Why did I feel so upset that my life was being turned upside down? Why were anger, bitterness, and resentment overtaking love?

Contrary to what I told myself, I am human. I am not capable of doing what only God can do. I am broken, living in a broken world. Emotions were human, but my actions would determine my allegiance: was I living for this world, or for the next? I knew I needed to pray for God to change my heart, and as I did, He gave me a clear picture of His ask of me: to surrender my independence and pride. To submit. To defer to Him. To trust Him.

* * *

In that closet, with my head on the scratchy carpet, I wrote a group text to Adam and four of my parents' best friends. "Dad is being released next week, and I can't do this. Can you help?"

Within seconds, each one replied with some version of the same thing. "Yes. When can we come over and plan?"

Unconditional love and support. With this response, those tears finally started flowing. I felt seen. I felt heard. When every thought in my head said, "You can do this yourself, don't bother people," my heart chose to ask for help. And it felt good. It felt so good. I realized as I stood up that my breathing had become shallow, and now I could take a deep breath again. I realized that my feet had been dragging and were now a little lighter.

God never meant for us to do life alone. That's why there are countless references in the Bible to church and family. So often we believe the lie that it is easier to be alone because we can run faster by ourselves than with a group. We can win the race alone. But God never calls us to that. He calls us to do life with others. Intellectually and spiritually, I believe we have different gifts and strengths that are complementary, not contradictory. When we live in community, our gifts and talents can be used to support and enhance one another. God gives people what they need, when they need it, and sometimes that comes through the gifts of those around you: of your community, your church, and your friends. Practically, my hands did not often follow my head. While I knew these things, it was and would continue to be a challenge for me to grapple with putting my thoughts into practice.

On a sunny Tuesday night, my army of supporters came over. Sitting on my couch while I handled a calendar on the coffee table, we made a plan. A plan that involved care for Dad, for Mom, and even for Adam and I. We ultimately decided that we needed a week to get our own lives together, and I would ask Laurel Place for an extra week of grace to keep Dad there, so that I could get his support system set up. He needed to go home, to his own house. And he would be alone without Mom there. So we scheduled sleepovers for the men at my parents' house to make sure Dad wouldn't wander, rides to and from the hospital on certain days, and rest time for Adam and I to be away from it all. We called on all the offers of support we'd had so far, and everyone delivered. His freezer would be filled with ready-made food by a parent of Carlee's former teammate. On that Tuesday night, those five people, whom I love as though they are my own family, saved my life. They made living a life possible, even if it wasn't the life I had envisioned, especially in my first year of marriage.

So with a plan in place, now I needed to tell Dad.

Telling Dad about the support structure we had wouldn't be the hard part. It was telling him that June 1 would come and go with him still living in Laurel Place. I delayed it for a week after we met with his friends, and on June 1, worked up the courage to tell him what was going on.

"Dad," I started. I was sitting on his single hospital bed while he flipped through the channels on the TV. Adam, my steady supporter, sat in the chair opposite.

"Honey, when do I go home again?" he interrupted.

"That's the thing, Dad, there's been a change."

Dad slowly looked at me, pulling his glasses up from his nose to his forehead, resting them above his eyebrows, and he started to cry.

I scooched closer beside him on his bed and continued. "Dad, I don't know if you remember me telling you this last week, but Mom is back in the hospital."

He nodded slowly. "Yes, with cancer," he replied.

"Yeah, and Dad, I just don't know how I'm going to take care of you yet at home without Mom there. I need a little time to get it sorted out and to get Mom taken care of in Abbotsford."

Very slowly, like the old man he had become since entering the hospital, Dad sat up. His shoulders began to heave as he started sobbing. He wouldn't open his eyes, as though he was trying to keep the tears inside of him. What he said next surprised me. "Okay, honey. I'll be okay. You go take care of Mom, and I'll be here when you are ready for me to come home."

I'd misjudged him. The man that had a traumatic brain injury and stroke had caught me by surprise. Maybe, just maybe, the nurse in the CSICU had been wrong; maybe his personality wouldn't change after all. Maybe I was right to tell the doctor and nurse back in the CSICU that he would be the same Rod he was before his stroke. This empathy and understanding was exactly who Dad had always been. Maybe a return to normal was on the horizon after all.

Mom's family on a special occasion. In front of Helen and Jake,
from left to right, are Mom, Cliff, Irene, and Bruce.

Despite becoming a "city girl," Mom's foundation in 4-H and
on the farm instilled a value of hard work and a belief that you are
never too important to get your hands dirty.

October 8, 1983. Rod and Emily married their best friends: each other.

Emily Quiring and Bonnie Bausenhaus, friends since Bible school and future mothers-in-law of the other's child. Forever each others' biggest supporter.

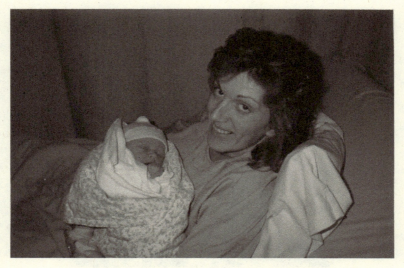

Emily first got to use the title Mom as she gave birth to me.
A title that would hold much more meaning as we both got older.

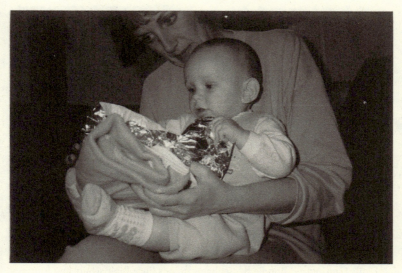

Her little boy, Cody, brought her so much joy.
His kind heart and sense of humour brought out the best in her.

Our family, at my grandparents' fiftieth wedding anniversary party. My shoes are undone because my feet hurt terribly, but that wouldn't stop us from celebrating with the extended family.

Disneyland was one of our first big family adventures. We went twice in two years, which was only possible because Mom got hotel discounts from her work with Marriott International. Always the leader, even if she didn't know where to go, she held our hands among the crowds and gave us the security we thought we needed.

First day of school, circa 1994. Note the epic 90s patterns and hair.

Mom and Dad were always my biggest on-court supporters. No matter my age, I always had one of them at every game or tournament. Even while I played for the UBC Thunderbirds, they came to every match, missing only the first national championship that we won. After that, they weren't going to miss any more . . . and we did win four more after that. They were there, faces painted and vuvuzelas honking, for every moment.

Her greatest gift was being Cody's Mom. She loved watching his intensity on the court, and his humour after. She'd buy him Subway, and he'd squeeze her with gigantic hugs. They were the yin to the others' yang. Even being two provinces away, she would fly out to almost every home game— claiming business reasons so she could get her flights covered through her company.

Our nuclear family grew with the addition of Carlee and Adam. We didn't realize how desperately we needed them in our mix. Carlee's patience and unwavering support kept us going, even when she couldn't physically be with us. Adam's steadfastness and lightheartedness balanced the crisis that would come after this day.

Our wedding was a day full of love and ignorance. If we'd known what we would face in the coming months, we'd be gripping each other even more tightly. We committed that day to walking life's trials together, and our vows were put to the test almost immediately.

My love and my life.

In 2014, Dad rode the Ride to Conquer Cancer from Surrey, BC, to Seattle, Washington. He rode 250 kilometres in two days in support of cancer research. His story was picked up by local newspapers and he was determined, at fifty-five years old, to finish at the top of the pack and fundraise all he could. He finished in the top 10% of riders overall.

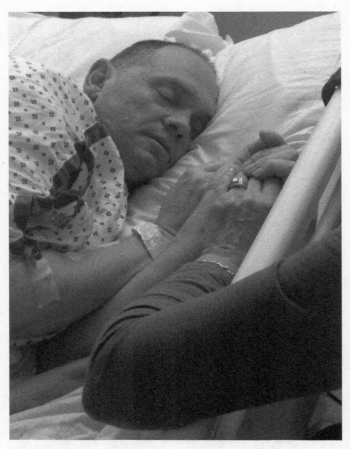

Dad in the Cardiac ICU. Even after they removed his ventilation, they kept him sedated for his healing. Mom was with him every opportunity she had, holding his hand and reminding him that she was still there. That she'd be with him, no matter the outcome.

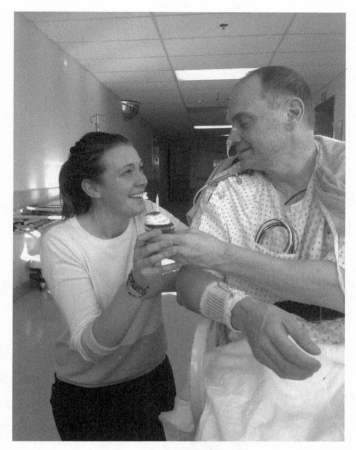

Dad collapsed on my twenty-sixth birthday, so we never got to celebrate the way we had intended. Once he was stable enough to move to the cardiac ward, Mom brought cupcakes, and we celebrated together. By every statistic, he should have died on my birthday instead of living to give me a cupcake a few weeks later.

Dad began to walk quickly and was stronger than the physiotherapists believed he could be after suffering such a devastating heart attack and stroke. He proved them wrong by walking a few days later, spending as much time as he could in the fresh air.

Dad's fifty-sixth birthday was also celebrated in a hospital. In Laurel Place, Mom brought him a Dairy Queen cake, and we sang to him. Later that night, he didn't remember his birthday, or that we had been by to celebrate with him, and he cried when we reminded him of what we'd done together. The memory impairment was taking its toll on all of us.

Daryl Edwards was as saint-like as a man with a dirty sense of humour and extreme sarcasm can be. He was constantly at Dad's bedside and taking him out for coffee. Without his advocacy with the hospital staff and friendship, Dad's healing would have been a much different story.

After three months in locked-down rehab, Dad was finally released to go home.

On a weekend pass, Mom and Dad took in a walk.
It would be their last one together.

Once he got home, Dad wanted to get back on his bike. He rode with Daryl
around the park, proving that miracles do happen.

After returning to the hospital with a lump on her head,
Mom couldn't be taken away from the Canucks.

The blind leading the blind. Dad couldn't remember where the visiting
room was, and the tumour in Mom's head was rendering her blind in her
left eye. So while he guided her, she gave directions. A marriage that
complemented each other time and time again.

97

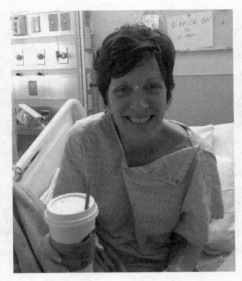

Mom, immediately following her brain surgery to remove her tumour. She looked so calm and peaceful for just having had a doctor inside her head.

Cheryl Simpson was an incredible friend and supporter during this season, and every one to come. She was Mom's confidante and levity. She gave Mom peace and eventually took on the role of Auntie to me and Nana to my kids.

Our last family photo, courtesy of Katie Wiskar.

Choosing burial plots for Mom. Dad struggled to be separate from her, so he stood where she would be laid to rest.

Dad's survival is a miracle. This smile is a marvel, his joy is God-breathed. He lived. He lives, and while the challenges continue to mount, he continues to fight.

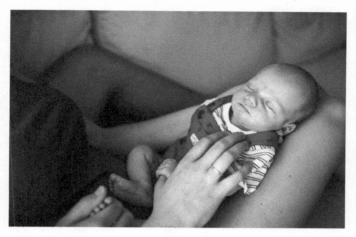

Knox, our precious firstborn.

Learning to be a mom without a mom was an unexpected challenge
that I was not prepared for.

These two brought me out of a significant depression. They showed me how to open my heart again to love, and how to recognize that love is always worth the cost of grief.

Savannah Emily, named after a woman as fierce and tough as she is.

This girl taught me that being your own person is okay. I'd tied myself to my mom's identity—we look the same and act the same. So even though Savvy and Mom share a name, they are their own person. There is no shame in loving your history and also using it to grow and be better.

Dad and daughter relationships are precious and terrifying. These two, like my own dad and I, balance each other out and bring out the best in one another.

Nothing can prepare you for becoming a mother. And being a motherless mother is terrifying and lonely. While Mom should have been here and could have been the best grandma, I am going to raise these kids to know her, to know God, and to know their own strength, because that is one genetic trait that will never be forgotten.

010: THE BLIND CAN SEE

In the days that followed Dad's release from rehab, we made every effort to get him to the hospital to see Mom. Most days, this started with Dad changing from his sweatpants to jeans and a button-down shirt because, in his words, "I have to look good for the woman I love." We would stop at the Starbucks in the hospital lobby, grab Mom's quad grande with room Americano with her ever-present, green plastic straw, and head upstairs to sit with her in some rather uncomfortable chairs.

Mom's Starbucks order will forever remain a thing of legend within our family and circle of friends. For years she would stop at the local Starbucks before work, before church, or before having any sort of intelligible conversation with anyone. The baristas began to recognize her black BMW and would start her drink before she even walked into the building. Quickly after discovering her new favourite drink, Mom realized that a straw in the cup would serve two purposes: keep the precious coffee from spilling out of the cup while she wove around traffic, and also keep her teeth from staining too much. Equal parts vanity and practicality. She was rarely spotted without her paper Starbucks cup in hand, and my cousin Jayme began referring to the drink as "rocket fuel" when she would order one in solidarity during her hospital visits to the family. Disgusting, yet accomplishing its purpose.

It's always astounding to me how we create habits and then hold them fast, even if they don't serve us the way they once did. Mom's coffee order is a prime example. In her working days, this rocket fuel order and supporting straw served a purpose, even if it didn't taste all that wonderful to me. But even when she got to the hospital, this was her regular mobile order. She probably shouldn't have had all the caffeine that was in there, and certainly didn't need a straw, given she was just sitting in her hospital bed, but this was what she wanted and craved. The habit was more than just the coffee order, though: it was the familiarity of what once was, of a time in Mom's life when she was at her prime. The coffee symbolized her success and her freedom. It symbolized her former life. In an attempt to hold on to what once was, she held on to this coffee. We all have our own Starbucks orders that we hold on to, even if we can't see them for what they are.

And sometimes, we just can't see anything.

Early in Mom's first admission to the hospital, when she was blind in her left eye, we broke Dad out of rehab jail and brought him to Abbotsford to visit. As was his custom on their visits, he dressed up and wanted to bring her coffee to her bedside. His plaid shirt hung loosely, just as her hospital gown did. As we sat down in the room, Mom began complaining that she was tired of looking at the purple walls and wanted to go for a walk. Dad, so impaired by a brain injury that he almost couldn't tell left from right, jumped up and quipped, "I'll take you wherever you want to go."

I tossed Mom one of Cody's old sweatshirts and she swung her feet out of bed. Her grippy socks were the same standard-issue hospital ones that Dad wore back at Royal Columbian. She put on the sweatshirt, and Dad grabbed her hand to help her stand. She slowly pivoted toward the door and remarked that she still couldn't see out of one of her eyes. Mom grabbed Dad's elbow, and together they began taking slow steps into the hallway.

One half blind, the other having no idea what direction they were going in. The blind was leading the blind.

Thirty-one years before, these two young kids walked up the aisle, Emily holding Rod's arm after promising to remain committed in all circumstances. I can safely say that this was not what they were expecting. They were not expecting to be blindly walking down the hallway, gripping each other for safety. They were certainly not expecting to be living in different hospitals in their early fifties, generally only communicating via pre-recorded video messages that their daughter would bring back and forth.

Love and marriage rarely end up looking the way you think they will. We grow up with pictures in our minds of what love and commitment look like. Sometimes relationships break and can hurt, if that's what you grew up with. In other cases, maybe it is a fairy-tale relationship that you have set in your mind: there will be no hurt, no conflict, nothing but long walks on the beach at sunset. My parents had always viewed their marriage as being one of friendship, health, and longevity. Yet what those of us who were watching saw in this moment was a marriage of fear and worry. But also one of unwavering support and commitment. It was a living testament to their vows and adaptability. A commitment to remain no matter the circumstances.

As Mom and Dad walked down the hallway together, toward the visiting room, my heart began to break. It broke because of their commitment to their vows to stick it out no matter what. It broke because of this act of love and service to one another. It broke because the situation felt so pitiful. Tears rolled down my cheeks as I recorded the slow shuffle down the hallway on my phone. This was marriage at its finest and its worst. And it was beautiful.

This was the example that my seven-month-old marriage had to look up to. Adam's and my first year together was indescribably chaotic and stressful, suffering something no marriage should have to go through, let alone so early together. But we stayed the course together.

* * *

As time would soon pass, the true picture of my parents' marriage was painted more fully for me. I wouldn't have said my parents were affectionate in the way that TV dramas define romantic. But what my parents had was teamwork. After thirty-one years, they knew how one another operated, how they thought. They knew how to handle each other's stress. Their love languages were second nature to each other. As much as Mom's volume of work frustrated Dad, he showed her unending support by taking care of us so she could do what was important to her. And when Dad's lack of self-confidence would rear its head, Mom would go out of her way to make sure he knew his value to her and our family, regardless of income or job title. Their marriage still came with regret and guilt for a variety of things, but that's what happens when two humans decide to spend and do life together. Some days, I think that they stayed together for Cody and I instead of out of love. In those seasons, I rarely saw affection between them, or even the hard conversations. But then again, I was usually in bed by 8:30 p.m. As the seasons turned, so did their reason for commitment.

* * *

For Mom's entire hospital stay, there were very few people she would let visit her in person. It was a matter of protection for her; she wanted to be in control of the image she put out to the world, and there were few people in her life who she would let see her with a bald head, in a hospital gown, or growing more emaciated each day. Plus, she wouldn't want to be rude and kick out a visitor when a doctor came in or when a nurse arrived to help her go to the bathroom. One of these lucky few who was allowed to visit was a relatively new friend from church, Dianne. She was tiny in stature, soft-spoken, and had the bounciest curls on her head. She was incredibly sweet, honest, and direct when called for.

Dianne began visiting Mom every few weeks, and one day offered to lead Mom in communion. In her purse, she had crackers and a little flask of port. Decidedly not the Welch's grape juice that was so common in the Mennonite church. She would hold Mom's increasingly frail hand, pray, and they would take the elements together. It soon became a regular tradition between the two friends, with others joining in as they were able and available.

For Mom, this became a huge source of comfort. As sure as she was in her faith, the discipline made it all the more real. This small act of eating a cracker and sipping port reminded her of the importance and surety of her salvation. The reason that she could have peace about leaving her family. For Mom, communion was a way of restoring her body and soul; she believed wholeheartedly that in symbolically eating and drinking the body and blood of Jesus, she was getting closer to her Saviour. Her confidence was in heaven, where she believed that her body and blood would soon be restored to perfect health.

011: MEMORIES BEHIND A PHOTO

Dr. Gurjal, Mom's medical oncologist, had come by her room for a serious chat. Cheryl and I had been updating Mom on some neighbourhood gossip when the doctor walked in with a small smile on her face. Cheryl was one of Mom's closest friends and an empath. She has almost endless empathy for everyone around her. Her time and energy were given with abundance. Yet she knows when to sit, when to listen, and when to speak. A gift that very few have. In this moment, she knew exactly what was coming and was prepared for the words Dr. Gurjal would speak.

"It's good to see you Emily, and to see you with your friends," Dr. Gurjal started.

"You too, Dr. Gurjal. It's been a while," replied Mom.

Then Dr. Gurjal got serious and laid out the situation. "Emily, you know that your cancer has spread. You know it's in your legs, your lungs, and your brain. We can do chemotherapy . . . that is still an option, but it will not change the end for you. It may prolong things, but the cancer is too deep in your body."

Mom nodded, no tears evident. She knew this was likely the news that was coming. But she asked anyway, "Can I please have some time to think about it?"

As Dr. Gurjal walked out of the room, Dianne walked in. She saw our sombre faces and quickly understood the stress she was walking into. Together, Dianne, Cheryl, Mom, and I grabbed hands and began praying. Dianne prayed for peace, for wisdom, and for healing. Despite the emotions of the moment, none of us cried. As we opened our eyes, we all knew the answer that Mom would give, and each of us felt a supreme confidence in it.

"I'm going to say no to chemo." And with that, Mom signed her own death certificate.

* * *

She woke up the next morning on a bright, sunny Saturday in the hospital and decided things would be different. Mom called me, chipper and earnest in her request.

"Rayel, bring me some nice clothes, my wig, and my razor. And grab food from the deli."

Shocked by this quick turnaround in her mood and energy, my mouth hung open. Just the day before, she had been told that her breast cancer had metastasized to her ribs, her lungs, her bones, and her skull. There was no place in her body this cancer wasn't touching. The doctor had bluntly told her that this was a matter of weeks, not years. Desperate to seize any piece of positivity I could get, my response was swift.

"Done. What do you want for lunch?"

As quickly as the phone call began, it ended. She had said her piece, made her wishes known, and, like always, we were to carry them out. It had always been this way with Mom; she was the manager and key delegator.

* * *

There was one Christmas when I was about ten or so when Mom's decisiveness and ability to delegate really made itself known. Christmas was Mom's holiday. She cared about every aspect: the tree had to be decorated perfectly, the dinners were to be gourmet, and the gifts were extravagant, even in the years when she and Dad struggled to pay the mortgage. On this particular Christmas, Mom had stretched the calendar thin, trying to have every family we knew over for their own special Christmas dinner. This meant that we had to get in line and get our tasks done twice a weekend to make sure we could execute this perfectly-planned dinner. It wasn't so much an exercise in hospitality for the rest of us as more of an exercise in efficiency and time management. But in the end, we always did it, and it always worked out perfectly.

This particular Christmas, I was assigned to napkin folding. There was even a manual. I kid you not. She had bought a book on napkin folding and brought it home for me to study, practise, and perfect before the guests arrived. She chose something my ten-year-old self could handle and ensured I pressed the napkins before I started folding. I was so frustrated; I wanted to be licking the brownie batter beaters or even tidying my room, because anything had to be better than the mundane task of folding napkins. But we all knew that when Mom delegated something, it had better be done, and done to the best of our abilities.

Perhaps those weeks in and weeks out of napkin folding taught me more than a physical skill, which I can still unleash when the moment calls for it. Perhaps it was a lesson in perseverance or in paying attention to the details. This could all be true, but when I think of that season, all I think about is hiding. Hiding the mess and chaos behind perfectly folded napkins. Hiding the work, the study, the frustration in the perfect creases and crisp folds. Hiding the realness behind what we want everyone else to see.

Or making decisions based on what we think others want. Perhaps this is why it felt so hard to make choices aligned with my values, like changing careers and becoming a coach. This need to cover who I am with what I think others want to see. It's scary to put yourself out there—emotions, fears, inconsistencies, and all. But haven't I been choosing courage this whole time? Why don't I have enough courage to show the world my true self? I feel ashamed that I have courage for so much yet not enough to simply be me.

Maybe this is why Mom dressing up in her nice clothes, wig on, and legs shaved brought back memories of Christmas. Wasn't she just hiding the brokenness and chaos? And why?

One rational answer is to mask her fear. To cover the catastrophe that was brewing inside her body. To protect her children and her husband from the reality that her body felt, even if her mind hadn't yet accepted it. Or perhaps, for one day, she didn't want to choose courage. She wanted to choose to pretend things were normal rather than brave the next storm to come her way. Sometimes it's simply easier to leave the beach than to continue fighting the waves.

Regardless, I went to Morenos Deli and picked up her turkey sandwich on pumpkin cranberry bread, bocconcini salad, and fruit platter. I packed her mustard-yellow pants, her striped t-shirt, and her new wig into her god-awful blue and green bag that we called the "flower bag," even though it had gaudy palm trees, not flowers, all over its soft sides. I think she'd won it at a golf tournament at some point. She didn't actually like it but used it because it was the right size and got a rise out of all of us. We all walked into the hospital: Dad, Cody, Carlee, Adam, and I. I left the family in the waiting room while I got Mom ready. The sun was streaming through her windows, and it lit up her eyes even more than a picnic lunch with the entire family did.

"Rayel, I got the nurse to bring a cardboard bucket for water so you can shave my legs." She was prepared, as always.

I got to work. As I dry-shaved my mom's legs, she put on her makeup, sitting in bed using a handheld compact. We didn't talk much, preferring to focus on our tasks, but at one point, we both looked at each other and started chuckling at the absurdity of it all. I never would have thought that I would be shaving my fifty-four-year-old mother's legs. And, I wondered, *Why didn't chemo stop that particular hair growth too?*

As we started to get her dressed, I quickly realized that without the use of her legs, getting her skinny jeans on was going to be a difficult and draining challenge. And even if we could get them on, we would only be taking them off to hop back into bed anyway. We struck a compromise.

"Mom, do you think we could just wrap your legs in a clean sheet, like a dress, instead?"

She was unimpressed and reluctantly agreed. As she settled her wig into place, I called the nurses to come and lift her into the wheelchair.

As I pushed her down the hallway, we turned the corner into a sun-filled visitor lounge where Dad, Adam, Cody, and Carlee had lunch all set up, with genuine smiles on their faces. Their eyes showed a mixture of relief and amazement; maybe there was a chance we could make this feel normal, even just for a few moments.

I think we needed a minute of normalcy. Our family culture was one where laughter and good food were central. And those had been missing for a long time. It wasn't often anyone could get a word in when we all sat around the dining room table, with at least three conversations going on at once. But in the past few weeks and months, silence entered where there had previously been no room for it. I think we all craved what was so we could strengthen ourselves for what would be. A grounding in the past and what made us strong.

Despite not having eaten more than small bowls of oatmeal for a few days, Mom's appetite seemed spurred by the delicious food. She ate more in that one meal than she had in a long time. We were so into our lunch and laughter that we almost didn't notice when my close friend Katie showed up to visit. She had the day off and wanted to come and check in on all of us. After a long drive from Vancouver to Abbotsford, she joined us for fruit salad. Katie is one of the most brilliant people I know, an internal medicine doctor who is regularly called upon to make sense of difficult research and diagnose the toughest of cases, all the while doing it with her signature compassion and sensitivity. And as she was devouring some strawberries with my family, she had her most brilliant idea to date.

"Can I take a family picture?" she asked.

Now, when you've been friends as long as we have, you know that a simple, six-word question can mean much, much more than what was just asked. Like when your bestie tells you that a dress looks "fine" instead of "great," you know that you should keep looking. I looked at my brilliant MD friend, and her eyes gave away what her training had taught her, and what she didn't want to say out loud: this would be the last time we would all be together. This unspoken sentiment was realized by us all. This *last family photo* became monumentally important.

We huddled up, arms and hands touching in all the ways we possibly could. Squeezes and cheeks touching. We smiled when all we wanted to do was cry. And that was that.

When I look back on those pictures now, I see something different in our eyes than I remember feeling that day. Mom's eyes are bright and clear, full of joy that her whole family was together. Dad's eyes and lazy smile are content, like he's safe where he is. We kids, the four of us, are surrounding our parents. Our arms protectively coming around each other and encircling the two ill ones. And we look resolved. Resolved to make the best of the worst situation. Resolved to hold our family together when our parents couldn't.

That's the way of life, isn't it? As one generation grows older, the younger steps up to care for them and to continue with family legacies, traditions, and responsibilities. I saw my parents do this for my grandparents, but my grandparents were old. They weren't in their mid-fifties. How were we, in our mid-twenties, supposed to take on this role when we were just kids ourselves? Were we really entering the sandwich generation so young? How could we possibly know what to do or have the capability or capacity to do what needed to be done? How were we supposed to parent our parents?

In hindsight, I realize now that God prepared me for this new role well before I ever had to take it on. As a child, I had a ridiculously good memory for events and experiences. While I couldn't necessarily tell you every random fact about volcanoes, I could verbatim tell you what happened at Grandma and Grandpa's house on a particular sleepover trip. I chalk it up to being a kinesthetic learner, but this was and is my reality.

Growing up, I also had a strong sense of responsibility. As the oldest, I felt it was my job to take care of my brother. This was both asked for by my parents and intuited by me. Cody would also say that I manipulated situations to get him into trouble and not me—and he wouldn't be wrong about that. I regularly blamed the messy bathroom on him. We both know it was my fault. But while my parents worked, I felt a clear calling to feed us and to make sure that we were ready for whatever activity that night had in store for us. Whether this sense of responsibility was driven by birth order or a feeling of intrinsic guilt, I'm not sure. However, caring for my family was always in my DNA.

* * *

God prepared me for this new role by giving me a resilient mother. Someone who could walk into rooms, seemingly devoid of emotion and able to command attention. Mom could find logic where emotion existed and make decisions based on fact, not feeling. So whether nature or nurture, this was also who I became. While I am highly emotional (thanks to my father's genes for that), I'm able to separate my emotions from my decisions in almost a clinical manner when the situation calls for it. I can excise the facts and postpone the emotions to make decisions driven by logic and reason. This skill, while not always healthy, allowed me to make tough choices and difficult calls in the care of my parents.

Mom also passed down her need for control. I, like her, try to curate information and access to it. I'm sure it's partially genetics, but it's likely mostly learned behaviour. And this behaviour continues to cause me problems and unintentionally cause hurt to those around me as I seek to quell my fear with control when I need to release it to others.

And for whatever reason, God also placed a gift of leadership within me. An ability to see the big picture, make decisions quickly, and bring others along on the journey with me, even if I have no idea where we are going. Somehow, and for some insane reason, people follow me. They assume I know what I am doing, believe in my confidence, and come with me.

A mentor once told me that when God gives you a gift or a strength, He never takes it away. Perhaps the gift is a trait. Or maybe a person. It is always there for you to draw on, to use when you need. It took this situation for me to realize that. My gifts came together for a clear purpose. Our people rallied with us to make the best out of a terrible situation. God has proven time and time again, both in the Bible and outside of it, that all things work together for the good of those who love Him. He used my flaws, my strengths, and my flexible three job situation to take care of my family, to protect those I loved, and to lead us all through one wicked storm after another.

* * *

After lunch, I wheeled an exhausted Mom back to her room and helped her get back into her anemic hospital gown, which drained the colour from her face the moment she put it on. I replaced her wig with her soft, grey toque but left her makeup on to make her seem more alive than she probably felt. As I turned to leave, she hugged me and whispered, "Does Dad know?"

"Yes," I responded. "He figured it out. He knows your pain and guessed that the cancer has jumped to your other leg."

As I started to tear up, she asked me to sit next to her. She began to stroke my face, my hair. My frizzy mess of hair was tamed by her fingers, putting stray pieces gently behind my ear. Then she raised both arms and held my face in her soft, swollen fingers. Then she started to whisper, "I love you. I am so proud of you. I am yours forever. You will never know how much I love you. No matter what you do, what mistakes you make, what accomplishments you have, or what you choose to do with your life, know that I could not be more proud of you. I will always be your mom, and I am so proud of who you are. No matter what happens, I will forever be yours, and you will always be my baby girl. You were my first, and I love you tons."

The tears flowed so fast that I couldn't see. My nose ran, and my sobs shook my whole body. These were the best words that she ever could have said. She asked if I wanted to lie down, head on her chest.

This woman, skin and bones with a huge chest from her reconstruction, laid my head down under her chin. Her skin was warm and soft, smelling like the Body Shop lotion that she had religiously used for years. We sat for a few minutes before she started stroking my hair again. Her right arm surrounded me in a motherly hug, and her left hand kept smoothing my hair. It was like I was a child again when she would calm me by playing with my hair. She continued talking,

"I love you. I love you."

"But Mom, I love you too! You are strong, a fighter, and so beautiful," I said, grasping for hope through any encouraging words I could find.

Her blue eyes were moist but determined. "That is who you are," she replied. "You are strong. You are beautiful. You are driven. I could not be more proud of you. You healed your dad, you know that?" With those words, my lungs gasped for air. Breath was hard to find.

"But Mommy, I wanted to heal you. I want you to get better."

She calmly looked at me, unwavering in her gaze. Sure of her statement. "It doesn't matter. You healed him because you love our family."

I felt torn. Guilty. Did she know that she meant as much to me as he did? "But Mom, I love you so much too. I am fighting so hard to save you too."

"I know, honey, but God saves us. We just are. I love you."

She never stopped stroking my hair.

"I love you. I am proud of you. I am your mom forever."

Sobbing, I begged, "Please don't leave me, Mommy. I don't know what I am going to do without you."

Ever so calmly, she replied, "You will be fine. You have Dad and Cody and Adam and Carlee."

"But I won't have you, Mom."

"You will always have me. I am a part of you. I am your mom forever and I love you tons and tons and tons. And I love the Lord, you know that. And because of that, I will see you again. Rayel, it's easier with hope."

And that was that. She sat with me for a time, all the while stroking my hair. Once my eyes had dried, it was on to the next conversation. The next person to hear from her. It was then that she asked me to send in our family members, one at a time.

For those dreaded conversations. The "I'm sorry I'll never see you grow up" conversations. Statements like "You've made me so proud." Sometimes those chats hold confessions or admissions that were withheld for so long. Or maybe requests for forgiveness. Absolution. I don't know what each of my family members heard from Mom that day, or whether they even remember it. Adam said he never got one. But my "I'll miss you" conversation didn't happen in one afternoon like it did for others in my family. It happened over the course of weeks. This was one of the perks of being around Mom so much. In each sleepover at the hospital, in each prognosis conversation with the doctors, in each report of how Dad was doing in rehab, that's when my conversations with Mom happened. That's when she shared her dreams for me and her memories of me. In those mundane moments, in the panicked moments, that's when we made our peace with each other. That's when we made our commitments to each other. In those terrifying days of worry and unanswered questions, we had our tough conversations, and we made little memories that I savour to this day.

And see, that's the thing. The dying are doing their best to create memories for the living. They are dressing up for pictures, they are eating when they don't feel like it, and they are having the tough conversations when they don't want to or don't know what to say. They are living for us, those who will remain, so we can have the best of the rest of them. But how we steward those memories is up to us. It is a tremendous responsibility.

012: ROLE REVERSAL

The sun streamed in the window that afternoon, illuminating the dust that was floating around the hospital room, just waiting to be caught by one of the housekeepers. It was oddly quiet, except for the occasional IV beep from down the hall. Mom was napping, with her mouth wide open, like she did when we went on camping trips in the summer.

After we moved to British Columbia, we often went back to Saskatchewan to visit family and take care of my grandparents the best we could. About five months after moving to BC, we went back to the prairie homeland for my grandparents' farm auction sale, where they were getting rid of everything from Mom's childhood property. But times were tough, and flying was out of the question, so we drove. Seventeen hours, straight. At six and eight years old respectively, Cody and I bunked down in the back of the truck, alternating sleeping in our quillows that Mom had hand-sewn, reading books, and playing our travel board games that Mom had picked up at the dollar store. Mom and Dad switched off driving duties.

When I think of that overnight road trip, two things come to mind. First, the entire truck being asleep while Mom was driving. I woke up in the back seat and peered over to the front. There was Mom, eyes wide like she was forcing them to stay open, two hands tightly gripping the wheel. I was old enough to read the speedometer and see that 160 km/h was maybe a little too fast. When I shrieked at our pace, I woke up Dad, who had more than a few words for Mom. But in her true, stubborn way, she told him to go back to sleep, and at this pace, we'd be in Medstead before he woke up again. The second memory turned into a core memory for me. A few hours after I played police from the back seat, Mom and Dad switched driving duties. In the passenger seat, Mom fell asleep in her usual way: head against the window, mouth open so wide you would think she was a frog catching flies. She would breathe so deep, tongue fluttering, but that mouth would never close. Nothing could wake her once she was truly asleep.

So when I saw that she was in her deep, wide-mouthed sleep at the hospital, I crept out to talk to the social worker. It was time to discuss options and what our next step was.

I can't recall the entire conversation, but I do remember that there weren't many options. Mom was done. She wanted to be comfortable. She wanted to manage her pain, and that was it. Chemotherapy was out of the question. Radiation or any more tubes were a nonstarter. She was tired of fighting, exhausted from the roller coaster of hope and despair that followed every meeting with a doctor. Rest was all she wanted. Location of that, whether here or heaven, was to be determined. As her healthcare representative, she asked me to make that clear to the social worker. I readied for a fight, to outline all our points and win any debate that was to be had. But there was no debate. The hospital accepted her decision with a mix of gladness and resignation. For me, this was a once-in-a-lifetime moment. For them, it was an everyday occurrence.

Where the debate did occur was whether she could stay at Abbotsford Hospital in palliative care or whether a hospice was the next best step. I was adamant that she should stay in the hospital. This was where Uncle Richard, my dad's brother, had died of cancer in 2009, so I knew what palliative looked like here. I didn't know what a hospice felt like, and, frankly, the idea of yet another change was incomprehensible. But as always in public healthcare, a lack of beds at the hospital made the decision for us. There were no palliative beds left. We would wait in her current oncology room until a hospice spot opened up in Langley. This could be as short as a few weeks, they said. With those papers signed and decisions made, I walked to Mom's room, dejected.

"Mom, now we wait. It might be a while, but they promised to keep you comfortable here."

"Well then, honey, you should go on your trip to Kelowna with Adam and your friends this weekend," replied Mom, always trying to make sure my life moved forward.

You see, that's the way she was. She knew that life doesn't stop for things like this, and I think that, in a way, she felt like this shouldn't be as all-consuming in my life as it was becoming. She knew that caring for my parents at the age of twenty-six and newly married was not the life I wanted, or the one that she thought I deserved.

"Are you sure, Mom?"

"Yes. But can you do me a favour? A promise, actually," she said.

I instantly became worried. My brow furrowed, and my eyes focused like lasers on hers.

She continued, "I am scared to go to hospice. Please make sure you're here when I get moved."

There it was. Her fear finally showed through the cracks of her always-tough exterior. We both began crying as I looked into her worried eyes. At that moment, she looked like a child, fearful of the monsters that were under her bed. Her breathing picked up, her hands began to shake, and she gripped my hand. I could see the panic beginning to set in, something I had never seen in Mom. Her hand clutched in mine and our foreheads touching, I breathed out my response. "I wouldn't be anywhere else."

Little did I know that Mom was becoming incoherent and confused again, much like when her brain tumour first appeared. It happened suddenly. She even told Cheryl, in her matter-of-fact way, "I'm going home on Friday." A statement made the day before she went to hospice that made all of us treat her even more like a child, questioning her ability to understand what was going on in her body and around her.

What was supposed to be a few weeks turned into a few days. Adam and I were barely in Kelowna for seventeen hours when she called with the news that she was being moved the next morning, a Tuesday. And, of course, when she called, she back-tracked on her request from the day before.

"Rayel, don't worry about coming home. Stay and enjoy the time with your friends."

"But Mom," I retorted, "you made me promise to be home."

I could hear her shake her head through the phone. "I'm fine. Cheryl and Bonnie are here, and I'll be just fine." It wasn't a true "I'm fine" but the one we all know means you aren't really fine.

I debated listening. The sun was warm. We had just got to the lake, and our friends and their parents were excited to spend a few days with us. I sat on the beach and cried, unsure of which of Mom's requests I should listen to. Adam reminded me gently that he would support me no matter what, but in his opinion, it was an easy choice. We should go home. Reluctantly, I agreed and, in that moment, I knew the end was near. I couldn't stop sobbing. I needed my parents. I needed someone to tell me it would be okay, to protect me from the inevitable. Adam could only fill this void so much. He'd been saying as much for months. Yet every time he said it, it seemed like things got worse. I couldn't bear to hear it again from him. Sometimes you just need your mommy and daddy.

It was my friend's father who stepped in. A man I didn't know all that well came over the sand and wrapped me in a hug. A long, hard hug where I fell into him, sobbing and shaking uncontrollably. He held me for what felt like forever, with one hand on my head. It was so reminiscent of what my dad would have done if he had been there and been his old self. There was a familiarity, a comfort to it. It was a moment where I felt that I didn't have to be the strong one, a moment where I was safe. I'll forever be grateful to that man for being there in those minutes, being that person for me.

We drove back to Langley in silence, Adam holding my hand the entire way, with only one hand on the steering wheel. He took us straight to the Langley Hospice and, while Adam figured out parking, I wandered inside. The social worker and nurse came out to greet me and walk to me to Mom's bed. The hospice was dark but air-conditioned on that hot July Tuesday, and eerily quiet.

Mom's room was just around the corner from the entrance. It was strange because it felt like a hospital, but there were no IVs beeping, no oxygen hoses coming out of the walls, and no sterile white lights everywhere. She looked peaceful, lying in her bed, covered in a pink blanket. In a moment of panic, I almost asked for them to remove the pink blanket: she hated pink because it represented both traditional femininity, which she strove to buck, and breast cancer, which she didn't want to acknowledge that she had.

She was sleeping, so after a quick kiss, I left her to meet with the hospice's social worker in the pseudo-living room at the front of the building. After showing me where the coffee, water, and snacks were, we got down to business. The social worker asked about Mom's favourite things: music, drinks, shows. Anything they could do to make her comfortable. They gently told me that they would do every-thing they could to keep her comfortable, but they would not be able to save her life. Numb, I nodded.

Then, as always in a business world, there was the matter of payment. The social worker at the Abbotsford Hospital had told me to make an application for financial assistance, so I asked the hospice to do just that. After gathering some quick biographical details, the social worker asked me for Mom's income. I gave them the number.

"So that's yearly then?" the social worker replied.

"No, that's monthly," I said.

She looked at me wide-eyed and closed her padfolio. "Yeah, she will not be qualifying for financial assistance." She chuckled quietly.

In hindsight, this might have been the one funny moment in the entire hospice stay. Of course my executive mother would not qualify for financial assistance! To think that her monthly salary could be construed as a yearly one was an indication of the immense privilege we'd been operating under the entire time.

That first day in the hospice was quiet. Adam went home to shower and bring some food back for us. Daryl had brought Dad to be with us. Mom sat there, staring blankly most of the time, with grunts coming out of her mouth here and there. Her words were confused, and the weakness in her body was completely different from when we'd left for Kelowna. But Dad sat there for an hour, holding her hand and talking to her like nothing was wrong.

"Oh honey," he whispered. "It's okay to let go. It's okay. I'll be fine. The kids are strong."

With that statement, he released her, absolved her of any more responsibility and gave the love of his life permission to leave him.

This, this was old Dad. The friend that would pick up the phone anytime I called in university, just to talk. The father who comforted and knew all the words to say. The husband who picked up the pieces when things were just about to fall and shatter. In that hour, there was no brain injury, there was no cancer. His personality was the same as it had always been. Even if it was just for a moment. This was the end of a thirty-one-year marriage built on love. It was patient, it was kind; it bore all things, believed all things, hoped all things, and endured all things. Even things that no one should have to endure. This love, this friendship, this marriage, endured it all.

Mom's words came back, and she started begging Dad, tears in her eyes and her voice anxious, "Please, take me home. I just want to go home!"

Dad, despite his brain injury, knew exactly the right words. "I know you do, honey, I know. The doctors just need you here a little while longer. You're safe, and this is where you need to be."

I couldn't answer. I could only cry. When your parent begs for you to keep them safe, how are you to respond? Dad begged in Laurel Place for me to take him home. Mom begged in Langley Hospice for me to change her outcome. How could I save them? How could I change things? My heart was so heavy. Mom told us she loved us. We let her sleep and promised to be back first thing in the morning.

True to our word, we were back before 8:00 a.m. on her second day in hospice care: Thursday, July 30. Mom had changed incredibly overnight. Words would not form. Her eyes would not focus.

"Can I feed you some breakfast?" I asked.

She replied, "Yes." I fed her two spoonfuls of porridge, and she wouldn't open her mouth for more. She clamped her lips shut like a baby refusing strained broccoli. I asked, "Is that good, Mom?"

She responded, "Yes, good. Thank you." And those would be the last words that Mom ever spoke.

That morning and afternoon, she slept. Sometimes peacefully, other times with strange breathing noises. Her face became waxy, and she started to stare at the wall, eyes wide, breathing with her mouth open but non-responsive. I remember the doctor coming in on Wednesday morning and I asked her how long she thought Mom had, because I knew Cody would want to be here for her last few days. He was likely going to come on the weekend anyway, which was only two days away. The doctor looked deep into my eyes and told me to call him now. In her view, Mom wouldn't make it until morning. Irene, Mom's sister, who is also a nurse and who had driven from Saskatchewan to be with us, agreed. Irene told me later that when she saw Mom, she was shocked at how bad it was and immediately called the brothers (Bruce and Cliff) to tell them that Mom was going and they wouldn't get a chance to say goodbye.

I panicked. I called Cody, and he wouldn't pick up, so I called Carlee next. Together we booked him flights for the next morning, to arrive in Abbotsford at 11:00 a.m. When he still didn't return my calls, I googled his work number and asked the receptionist to speak with him. I told him the news, and he lost it. Tears, wailing, and then silence. The silence became deafening.

Back in Mom's room, I told her that Cody would be here the next day, on Friday. Her little boy would be here, and he wanted to see his mommy. There was a grunt, and her eyebrows lifted. I told her I loved her, and she replied in the same way, with a grunt and eyebrow raise.

We thought hospice care would be peaceful, with wine, long summer days, and good conversation to finish out Mom's life. As usual, our expectations were completely wrong.

013: RELEASING IT ALL

She was only there three days.

The night before, no one slept. We kept listening for her breathing to change, for her to make noise, or for lighting to strike. Anything to tell us that this was going to be the end. Every time her breath laboured, I jumped to her side and woke everyone in the room, thinking that was her final moment. Every time the old man in the next room farted, I jumped up, thinking *that* was the symbol of the end. Imagine . . . a stranger's fart the indication that death was happening.

I sat next to her, holding her hand and taking pictures of our fingers intertwined: some of those nostalgic photos to look back on and probably use in a social media post to mark some stage of my future grief. I prayed and read the Bible, but if I'm honest, it was more for show than anything. Maybe if I acted like a good Christian, then maybe I'd feel peace, and maybe, just maybe, God would provide a miracle. But deep down, in that place that you don't really want to go because you know it'll hurt, I was mad at God and desperate for anything that might keep Mom around. I prayed for miracles so we could show the world His power, and I prayed that we would use this miraculous healing story to bring glory to Him. But in the end, it was for selfish reasons: I just didn't want Mom to leave.

* * *

When the sun came up on that sunny Friday morning, I could finally see the reality of what we were facing. The light reflected off her papery skin. Her eyes were vacant, as though she was seeing something we couldn't. Her cheeks were hollow, and her arms, so thin, splayed in awkward directions. She wasn't tracking our voices or our movement with her eyes or head. Her grey toque covered up her scars and her baldness but couldn't cover the absentness that I knew was in her brain. But those fake boobs? Those were still perky. They made her hospice gown sit like normal, but also accentuated the frailness of every other part of her body. The sun, that beautiful warm sun, brought to light everything that I didn't want to face. Adam told us later that it was one of the most beautiful sunrises he'd ever seen.

Nothing changed until late morning when Cody arrived. He rushed into the room, throwing his bag and ignoring everyone else. He pounced on his mother, sobbing, holding her hand and gently kissing her cheek.

We spent the next three hours together. Dad, Mom, Cody, Adam, Cheryl, Irene, Bonnie, and I. We read scripture, talked, and sat in silence. Each time we said something moderately funny, Mom's eyebrows would raise ever so slightly. Every time we told her that we loved her, she grunted back. But her stare never left the wall in front of her.

Around 2:00 p.m., her breathing became extremely laboured. It sounded like she was choking. Her eyes widened, and she fought. She fought with her body and her mind. She fought the feeling of choking.

We all sat there, sobbing around her. We kept telling her, "It's okay. You're going to be okay. We are going to be okay. Don't fight it. It's time." We said these things over and over again as she continued fighting for every breath.

All of a sudden, she grunted, and her breathing got even worse. She looked directly at Cody, deep into his eyes and breathing hard.

For about two minutes, she looked at him as he told her, "Mom, it's okay. Don't worry, you're okay. I love you. I love you."

Then she turned to me. Her head tilted, eyes huge, and breathing difficult, she stared at me. She grunted through her laboured breathing, and she stared, willing me to understand the message coming through her eyes. We have the same eyes. The same colour, same weariness, same way of communicating with them. I knew what she said, so I said it back with my voice.

"Mom, it's okay. Jesus is here. I love you. I'll always be your little girl. I love you, Mama Bear. I'm yours."

Then she took her last turn with Dad. With her eyes portraying urgency, terror, and desperation, she stared at him and her breathing got worse.

"I love you, honey," said Dad. "Rest. We will be okay. I will be okay. I love you so much. I love you, honey."

I moved from the end of her bed to her side, holding her left hand. As I moved, her breath got loud, and the choking sound became more intense. Finally, at 2:35 p.m., she took her last, very laboured breath, surrounded by her husband, her son, and her daughter. In the room were her son-in-law, sister, and two best friends. Mom left this earth surrounded by the people who loved her most and knew her best.

Immediately, Cody started to scream. Dad's tears were silent but streaming, and my lungs were unable to get enough air. I kept kissing her cheeks and putting my head to her hands. My brain grabbed hold of the physical world, yet again, in an effort to protect myself from the flooding emotions that I could sense were coming. Did you know bodies get cold immediately? Did you know that you can die with your eyes open?

It was Friday. Exactly as she'd told Cheryl when we questioned her mental state. Her prophecy was true. She went home.

Our pastor arrived about five minutes after Mom died. He came into the room and prayed with us that God would open the gates of heaven to Mom, claiming her as His child. We thanked God for faith and a life that was lived for Him. Her life. It felt strange to so quickly put her life into the past tense. Then we sang. In our terrible voices, tears cutting through every word, we sang "10,000 Reasons" by Matt Redman, choking on the lyrics that talk about praise amid death.

Adam left the room immediately, walking outside to get air and wanting to remember Mom as alive, not dead. Cody and I slowly followed, each needing to process and let our own circle of support know what had happened. My first call was to Jayme, my cousin.

"J," I started, struggling to speak even with her nickname on my tongue. "A few minutes ago . . ."

I couldn't breathe. I couldn't finish. And like the sweet, connected soul she is, she knew.

"Ray, I love you, and I am so, so sorry that Emily is gone. Can I pray for you?" and she did, right there on the phone.

In those early minutes, I'm not sure who else I called or who I texted. I'm not sure how I broached it or what was said. Shock does that to a person. It puts you on autopilot mode and allows you to still function without having any conscious thoughts or appreciation for what you are actually doing. It prevents you from processing. Shock robs the wind from your lungs and numbs your brain, to keep you from the pain that is sure to come. I was grateful for it. Because the idea of handling anything more in that moment was more than I could tolerate.

I couldn't handle anything else. The words of others, their prayers, washed over me like water, but with no reaction. Processing what to do with the body and the donations of her corneas elicited nods from me instead of actual words. Lighting the in memoriam candle in the lobby of the hospice brought on no tears. I was numb and wanted to stay that way.

The funeral arrangements began almost immediately. The planning was a way to take my mind off the trauma that we had been through the past number of months. Details came fast and furious, with decisions being made without consulting anyone. Mom didn't care about her funeral or what happened. There were no requests made, and no directives given. The one thing she gave up control of was her funeral. It was our grief to bear, not hers. I'm sure it drove my brother and dad nuts, but I was in the zone and kept going with it. Family showed up and just took care of things. My wonderful cousin Pam flew in with hugs and used my kitchen to make our grandma's favourite cinnamon twists. My father-in-law went to the store and bought a tub of mayonnaise when we only needed a tablespoon. My aunt Irene was the communications godsend for getting the details out to family. My sweet friend Kyla, who had lost her own brother a year earlier, took over my text and social media messages because the idea of responding to so many people who loved me was overwhelming. She knew this grief all too well.

I had so many family, friends, coworkers, and acquaintances who reached out during that time to express their sorrow and sympathy that Mom had died. They shared their own memories and their own tears over her life. I couldn't handle it. I couldn't handle their grief as well as my own. They had the best of intentions, and in reading the messages months later, I felt so deeply loved and known. But in the moment, it was overwhelming. I needed silence. I needed someone like Kyla to filter the well-intentioned noise and create a space of quiet for my emotions.

My grief needed silence to sit in, to grow larger in. My grief needed a place to yell where no one else was yelling. It required my tears as water to grow to the fullest that it could be. These feelings needed space to hide so that my brain could work on other things. It became as much a part of me as my arm or leg, and it had needs just as those appendages did. This grief became a limb that would not stop aching for a very, very long time.

* * *

On August 7, 2015, we woke up to an overcast sky and a warm breeze. I slowly got myself dressed in a new, deep purple Calvin Klein dress and put on all the waterproof makeup that I could find. Methodically, I packed my clutch with lipstick, tissues, and deodorant. I sat on the side of our bed and looked at my feet, captured in my own thoughts, until Adam touched my shoulder and ushered me out the door.

When we arrived at the cemetery in Fort Langley, the sun was beginning to break through the clouds, and the sleeveless dress I was in started to seem like a good idea. The funeral director guided Cody, Dad, and me over to the casket, and as we stood there, they opened it for us. Our shoulders all began to shake at the same time as we saw the woman we loved lying in her navy-blue dress in a satin-lined coffin. It might have been her body, but she wasn't there. The energy that gave her life was missing. The mortician's makeup could only do so much, but it would not make her who she had once been: a woman who grabbed life and made it her own.

Witnessing my mom's siblings walk by her coffin was a sight I will never forget. Auntie Irene was stoic, holding her tears back as she saw her childhood best friend and sister lying there. She intimately knew grief and loss, as her husband had passed away a few years before. Uncle Bruce, Mom's oldest brother, was the family empath, and it came out strong that morning. As he looked over his baby sister's body, he wept. The person he grew up protecting and teaching was gone. Uncle Bruce and Mom were incredibly close, and to him, it would have felt like a piece of himself was now gone forever.

The graveside service was simple and beautiful, with hymns sung by more close friends and a simple message from her pastor. It was exactly as she would have wanted: focused on God and quick. After the service, we drove to the church and prepared for the larger funeral and reception.

The church was dimly lit, and the music played softly in the background. From the chapel behind the main sanctuary, we could hear the sounds of people coming in and making small talk as they waited for the service to begin. The processional music began to play and, as a family, we got ready to walk in. As we walked down the dark aisle toward Mom's picture on the screen at the front of the church, I realized just how surrounded we were. We were hand in hand with family, friends surrounding us on every side, and Mom and Jesus looking down on us. It was a physical representation of our emotional state: there was not a single part of our family that was not surrounded by love. We were no longer lonely in our grief; those who knew her shared it with us and took a burden from us.

I was self-appointed to deliver the eulogy. In hindsight, I don't know why I decided that I was the best one to do it, other than to show people that despite my grief, I could be strong like my mom would have been. It was likely pride that forced this decision, and I didn't give others a chance to counter my decision. After Cody and Dianne shared some scripture, I walked to the front of the stage to deliver a story that I hoped would honour her.

* * *

Welcome to you all. I don't want to admit that I'm in shock at how many people are here today, but it is clear that Mom touched many lives. She would never have wanted to have everyone make a fuss over her, but we are so happy you chose to join us in this fuss. On behalf of the family, thank you. Thank you for sharing your life with my mom, for building into her life and for supporting our family. Even if we don't get a chance to speak with all of you today, please know that we are thankful you made it here to celebrate with us. In the bulletin, we have provided you with a history of Mom's family and a summary of her life. Most of you have probably already read it so I won't repeat it. Instead, I wanted to share with you some memories of Mom.

My name is Rayel and I am Emily's daughter. At least once a week for the last twenty-six years, I have heard someone end a sentence with ". . . just like your mom." Maybe it's "you are so organized, just like your mom" or "you are a 'leader' just like your mom" or, my personal favourite, "you look just like your mom!" Sorry, Dad, but I think that's a good thing!

So how do you begin to write a tribute to a woman who you share everything with—your looks, your personality, and your life? How do you share memories of a mom who valued faith, family, and friends above all else? How do you do justice to a mom who sacrificed everything so you could have more than enough? This is an impossible task, but there is one event that can at least help you understand Mom's values.

Christmas.

Christmas at the Quiring house was always quite the affair. And Mom managed it all. I think the Christmas tree was one of her most treasured Christmas traditions.

The entire family would go to Dogwood Christmas Tree farm, and Cody and I would get to pick out our favourite tree. Not that we could ever agree on one, so Dad would just take the saw to the closest one to the entrance. But when we got it home, that was Mom's domain, and no one else was allowed to touch it. The rest of us would get to take out the decorations from the crawlspace and Mom would go to work—ribbon, beads, ornaments. For anyone that ever saw one of Mom's Christmas trees, you would agree that it was absolutely perfect. She took pride in all that she did, wanting to give her kids a storybook Christmas every single year.

Then there was the Christmas lights. It would always start in early December, with her politely asking Dad to put up the lights. This would escalate to her not so politely asking and, finally, bribing with baking. The rule in the Quiring house was that for every string of Christmas lights Dad would put up, he would get one batch of baking. Our house always seemed to have an excess of lights . . . but Dad, I don't know if you knew this, but Mom always had double batches of everything for you, even if you wouldn't put up the lights. She loved you, and she showed it with food. She always showed love with food. You can ask the countless volleyball players she cooked for, the people she prepared meals for at Single Mom's Day at church.

But her Christmas baking topped it all. This was one of my favourite parts of Christmas with Mom. Every year, we would go through the cookbooks together, settling on eight or nine treats. Oreo cookies, Elsie's brownies, peanut butter squares, cinnamon twists, and Grandma Isaak's butterhorns were always at the top of the list. It's not the endless dishes or recipe following that I remember, but her reminiscing about her child-hood and parents while we baked. Heritage, she always said. You are so blessed to have such a great heritage and don't forget it. Look to your family for examples on how to live; they've done it right.

Hospitality and generosity were important components of Emily's Christmas Extravaganza. I remember one year we had a different family over for eight nights in a row, where Mom would make at least a four-course meal. Each person at the table would get a Christmas Cracker and a gift. Mom's house was open to anyone, as long as you would agree to eat. It's no wonder Mom spent so much time in the service industry. I remember her spending hours picking out the perfect bottle of wine to give to her team for Christmas, and being so proud of the Christmas parties her company would throw for its staff. Mom gave of her heart, and her wallet, with abandon. I have so much, why wouldn't I share with others? she would offer every single Christmas.

And then there was the Christmas Eve service at church, right in this very sanctuary. This was the most important part of Mom's Christmas season—it blended faith and family, the two biggest values in Mom's life.

Mom once told me that she would be happiest on Christmas Eve. The Christmas Eve that was to come.

*The one where her entire family would surround her,
all four of her kids and Dad, with his arm around her
shoulder. She told me that she wanted to sing "Silent
Night" and look down the row and see her heritage,
her legacy, and the product of everything she has ever
wanted. She wanted grandkids on her hip, praising
Jesus with her. She wanted us—her future—to love the
Lord the way she did.*

*Mom, you have taught us so much. You taught us how
to love, how to share, and how to give with our whole
hearts. You taught us to love the Lord and to rely on
him no matter what the circumstances. You taught us
how to be strong, independent, and determined.*

*Mom, I'm going to repeat the same words that you gave
to me in the hospital: I love you, I am so proud of you,
and I will always be your daughter.*

* * *

As I walked back to my seat, I felt a weight lifted. It was a significant
step in my journey of grief to deliver that eulogy. Maybe, I thought,
now that my obligatory to-dos were done, I could move on, and
things would get easier. I'd done the requisite things, processed
appropriately, and checked the boxes. That's all grief was, right? A
series of boxes and seven steps you apparently go through? That's how
TV and books made it seem. I hoped that maybe by doing things,
grief would be less. I was very, very wrong.

The service continued with heartfelt tributes from family and
friends, including Cody. After a brief message, we dimmed the lights

and had a time of communion during our better-than-our hospice rendition of "10,000 Reasons." As we stood to worship, our hands lifted and our eyes wept. We were mourning the loss of Mom and also celebrating the power of the resurrection. I believe, and I know that Mom and I will hug again and talk again because of the power of Jesus and what He did for us by dying on the cross. I can be sure of this.

The part of the day that Mom would have been so excited about was what we called the after party later that evening. We asked our family and close friends to join us and raise a Stella, her favourite beer, to Mom at the local pub. We had rented out most of the restaurant, and about fifty of us joined together to laugh and remember the best of who Mom was. She would have loved every second of it: people happy and celebrating her memory, rather than lamenting her absence. The after party was loud and boisterous until Adam let out a whistle, and Dad stood up to give a toast. The room fell silent as they listened to a broken man give tribute to the woman that made him a husband and father, to the woman who made him whole. His words captivated us all, and there was not a dry eye in the room when he finished.

* * *

To my family and friends gathered here today, I would like to offer, on behalf of Emily and myself, a toast. A toast to family and friendships. It's because of all of you in the room that we made it through the last twenty months. You have proven time and time again your love and your support for our family. You know that family means everything to me, and to Emily, so thank you for all being a part of our family—blood related or chosen.

And now, Emily, I have thought of this day for a while now, about how painful it might be to lose you. You are my best friend, the love of my life, and the mother of my children. You truly are my better half, and I'm glad the kids look like you. God was so gracious to give you to me for thirty-two wonderful years, and I'm jealous that he gets you from now on. I love you, always will.

If you will, please raise your glasses for one last toast to my beloved Emily—a woman I will never stop loving and missing. To Emily.

014: BLAME GAME

Well-meaning people will tell you that grief is different for all of us. That there are seven stages that we all walk through at our own pace, and that you will eventually come out the other side. What they don't tell you is the absolutely, completely overwhelming physical pain that grief invokes. That when you grieve so deeply, you can't catch a full breath in your lungs, no matter how hard you try. That there is an ache that goes down so deep in your bones that you can't shake it. That your eyes refuse to focus, partially because of tears and partially because the thing you want to focus on is no longer there. And that your memory becomes clouded to protect you from being overwhelmed. Yet all you can think of is the "woulda, coulda, shoulda" moments: those moments that were supposed to be, that were dreamed of, that were promised, yet will now never happen. And that any requirement to talk to people about what you are going through, or to respond to those well-meaning text messages, requires a herculean effort of both your brain and your thumbs.

After her death, my body betrayed me. Sleep, something I needed much of, eluded me for years. The nights became long. My mind wouldn't stop whirling. The last thing my brain would yell before falling asleep was "Mom!" It was like my soul was calling out, trying to find her in an empty space. A space she wouldn't return from. While my mouth didn't physically scream out each night, for years my brain would cry out right before I would go to sleep, longing for her to enter the room or my dreams.

Then my memory failed. For my entire life, my memory has been astounding. I can recall the colour I was wearing on my first day of school, or the colour of the blanket on the guest bed in my childhood home. The song from my Grade Two Christmas concert is burned into my subconscious. But in the weeks that followed Mom dying, I couldn't remember anything about my life with her. The trips to Disneyland became a fact with no feeling or detail associated with them. The Easters became a blur; all I could remember is that they happened in spring sometime. I couldn't remember her latest hair colour, let alone the words she spoke to me at the hospital, the words I so desperately wanted to cling to. Grief masked the memory. To save me the pain, my mind caused more.

And my body hurt. Every bone, every breath ached. It was a deep ache, yearning for something that wasn't there. Even after the tears were gone, my body felt hollow. I remember being in Disneyland after her funeral with the women that I coached, and my feet literally wouldn't pick up off the ground. I was so excited to be there and running around, but my grey Chuck Taylors kept catching on the sidewalk. My feet wanted to stay where they were, just as my heart and mind did. I didn't want to move on. And now and again, it would get caught in memories that I'd tried to forget, like one conversation Mom and I'd had a few months before.

* * *

"Rayel, you are the reason that your dad is alive."

The words abruptly came out of nowhere, the tone flat. Mom was scrolling her emails in her hospital bed, acrylic nails tapping her screen ever so quietly, and I was texting in the chair beside her. I looked up, caught completely off guard. It was a nondescript day, sometime between entering Abbotsford Hospital for the second time and her bone scan.

"What do you mean?" I replied with tears starting to form in my eyes.

And just then, the nurse came in to adjust the beeping IV drip, and Mom never answered my question.

In the months and years that followed, I regularly returned to that off-the-cuff comment from Mom. What did she mean? Was it a statement of gratitude that my dedication had somehow rescued her husband from certain death? Or was it a statement of resentment that my love for her wasn't strong enough to keep her alive?

I flip flop between what I believe those short words mean. In some ways, I know she was proud of the commitment and love I gave to Dad: showing up every day to walk him to coffee, answering the phone so often at work just to have the same conversation time after time, and fighting for him to have access to the best care we could find. I never gave up on him, and Mom and I both knew it.

We both knew that I prayed for him to get better and that I used every ounce of my strength to stay positive. We knew that I had sleepless nights because I was worried, and would spend hours and hours working with him at rehab. We knew that I spent 100% of my energy on helping him recover. In contrast, had I spent as much of myself willing her to heal? If I had been there more, prayed for her more, or fought for her more, would she be getting better? Was there something more I could have done?

These questions continue to plague me. Did I unconsciously make a choice of which parent to save? If you'd asked me to choose a parent as a kid, I'd have chosen Dad as my favourite. So did I play favourites here too, and choose him to save? That doesn't mean I didn't love her. I loved her incredibly much. But did I unintentionally choose? Could I have done something to keep them both alive?

Logically, I know the answer is no. Their stories, written and edited. God knew what was going to happen. I believe that there is, and was, a reason that Dad survived and Mom didn't, even though I can't understand it now.

But deep down, in a place of my heart that is so secret I try to hide it from even myself, I wonder. I wonder if it was my fault. I wonder if I could have changed the outcome. Mostly, I wonder if I am to blame. Because blaming myself is easier to stomach than blaming God. It means that there is a reason this all happened, and why the suffering continues.

That's one of the problems with death. Unasked questions plague your mind just as much as unanswered ones do. So we sit in our imaginations, wondering all the "what ifs" and "coulda beens" and "shoulda beens." We give answers to things that we shouldn't because we don't truly know what the other person would have said or done. I'm sure Mom wouldn't have ever meant or said that I chose Dad over her. But in the absence of any clear answer before she died, that's what my heart sometimes believes.

* * *

In the months that followed, my brain became tormented by the "what ifs." And the "oh she'll nevers." And the "we should haves." Every permutation of my past and my future was laid out there for inspection, for judgement. Did I do enough? Did I say enough? Should I have had kids at sixteen just so Mom could have become a grandma? Yes, even thoughts like those crept into my mind. The worst thoughts, though, were the "she'll nevers": She will never experience being a grandma; she will never travel back to Australia like she did with Kurt, Bonnie, and Dad as a twenty-something. Her contracts with clients will remain unfinished. The most painful "she'll nevers" that came to mind were selfish: She'll never be there to help me through labour. She'll never be there to save the day when the kids are cranky. She'll never host Christmas dinner again. She'll never take care of Dad. When it came right down to it, it was more about what I was losing rather than what she would never experience.

Because I believe that she is experiencing something greater. I believe that she is with her parents, and her sister who was stillborn, with Jesus in heaven. She is worshipping God, drinking the good wine, and celebrating every day that she is in the presence of God. She chose the gift of eternal life. She chose a life of faith that would lead to a life of eternity. Because she found Jesus, she certainly wasn't living in an eternity of regrets, what ifs, and never wills.

But I felt like I was stuck in that place. Adam began to worry that I would never come out of it, that I would be stuck in a cave of emotion forever. And I started to wonder if loving was worth it at all. Why love someone if they are just going to be taken from you? There's inevitable hurt and pain that comes with the joy of loving. In behavioural economics, they call it loss aversion: the pain of losing something is twice as powerful as the pleasure of gaining. And my loss aversion is high because I love deeply. Incredibly so. The deeper I love, the more I have to lose, the more it stings.

As the fog slowly began to subside and my brain emerged from the dense cloud it was in, I began to think logically and rationally about it. I didn't want to not love—that sounded like a cold world—even if it meant protecting my heart from breaking again. If I hadn't loved Mom, then I wouldn't know this pain: that was true. But loving Mom meant that I also felt love in return. It wasn't that Mom's love was conditional on me loving her first. But loving her meant I felt the fullest expression of the word. The warmth, the protection, the unconditionalness of it all.

Love is both a joy and a risk. We are called to love because God first loved us. It is equal parts a response to a good Father's love and also a responsibility, a commandment. To be vulnerable and to love with your heart, mind, and soul requires risk. You will have your heart broken, and there will be sadness. But that doesn't take away the goodness of it. It makes it more worthwhile. It hurts like hell when you lose love, when you feel that it was inexplicably taken from you. And those moments of deep love, forgotten in your grief. Moments of God-ordained conversation and Spirit-filled laughter. Those are the sweet memories that live on and make the loving worth it. The reward is greater than the risk, even when sometimes, at the end of the day, all you feel is sadness. Loving Mom for twenty-six years was not enough, and it still doesn't feel like the love we had was more than the sadness I feel in her loss. But twenty-six years of hand holding, hair stroking, and deep hugging are slowly starting to come back to mind, seven years later, and fill the deep void that she left behind. Without feeling her love and knowing her love for me, I wouldn't know the sadness. But if I didn't know her love at all, that would be a tragedy of epic proportions.

There were moments when I questioned the logic and math of what was happening to my family. There was an 11% survival rate for someone like Dad, who had a stroke and heart attack outside the hospital. But he lived. He survived, different from who he was before. The five-year survival rate for breast cancer patients is 90%. She was supposed to live. So why? Why did Dad survive and not Mom? Why did the odds completely work in reverse for our family? These are questions that haunt me and for which I will never have the answers. So I try to forget them, to move past them, knowing all the while that when answers are given, I will be staring into the eyes of Jesus, with Mom at my side in heaven.

015: NORMAL IS NUANCED

There is a lie out there that I feel compelled to dispel. There is absolutely nothing normal about what happens after someone you love dies. A new normal doesn't exist. There is no "standard" grieving process. Timelines for when you'll feel anything but broken vary. Nothing is relative because there is no comparison to what you feel: everyone grieves differently, and there's absolutely no way to predict what you will feel and when. There really is even no way to describe the days; there are no specifically good or bad ones. Every day that passes is one in which you are desperately trying to hold on to any semblance of reality that you can. Where you try not to spiral into the traumatic memories or the what-ifs that lead to pools of tears.

There's no acceptable timeline for anything. Deadlines mean nothing, and standards of when things are appropriate are relevant only to you. In my case, a vacation to an all-inclusive in Mexico nine days after Mom died felt like the right choice, though there was flak given to me by others, to be sure. Valid comments perhaps, in retrospect, though I own my decision and am glad Adam and I went anyway. In contrast, my grandma trying to set up my dad on a date with a fellow widower three months after Mom died did not feel like the right choice to me.

Was this also what the first year of marriage was like for everyone? Adam and I had rings for a grand total of 293 days, or ten-ish months. All of this happened before we'd even celebrated our first anniversary. That honeymoon phase ended quickly. We knew this wasn't what many went through, but I think it was only years later that we only realized how far from normal this was.

And then the "special" days hit you like a ton of bricks: the birthdays, the Mother's Days, the first anniversary of their death. They come out of nowhere, despite you knowing they are on the calendar, and surprise you with the depth of emotion they elicit.

Christmas was, as you know, the highlight holiday in the Quiring house. So it was expected that the first Christmas without Mom would be a doozy. Doozy was an understatement. Cody and Carlee were coming home for Christmas 2015, and we didn't want Dad to be alone. I made it my mission to make it as "normal" a Christmas as possible. As close as I could to a Mom-executed holiday, yet without the folded napkins. But as I've said, there is no normal. I felt this impossible task to take on the role of Mom, to fill her shoes and do what only she could do. I posted on Instagram a picture of her famous homemade Oreo cookies with this caption:

> *You look just like your mom. You bake just like your mom. You are exactly like your mom. Emily Junior. You are going to be a leader just like your mom. You are stubborn just like your mom. Did you know that you remind me of your mom? All these things I hear on a daily basis. When I was younger, these comments used to drive me nuts. Why couldn't I just be Rayel, separate from Emily's daughter? I'm realizing that I will never be separate from Mom. And I love that. I'm glad I can remind people of her, I'm glad that when I look in the mirror I start to cry because sometimes I see her looking back at me. I'm glad that her recipes will continue to bless people, even if they will never taste as good as when Mom made them.*

I felt this immense pressure to be just like Mom that Christmas. To bake like her, to host like her, to buy gifts with her extravagance, and to decorate with her flair. I was trying to bring her back in any way I could, to lessen the emptiness that her absence had brought. I did all the things, we celebrated all the ways, and still the holiday felt hollow.

There is simply no way to replace what can't be replaced.

And I was so wrapped up in myself that I didn't notice what the others needed. I assumed I knew what should happen, not recognizing what they might have wanted or hated. It is more than likely that I made their Christmas worse by trying to make it the same.

When her birthday rolled around in February, I tackled the grief in a very unhealthy way. I got absolutely hammered. I drank too much of her favourite red wine and finished with some limoncello. Mom had become obsessed with limoncello when she and Dad went to Italy to celebrate their twenty-eighth wedding anniversary. They couldn't go for their twenty-fifth because there was a volleyball game that week, so they chose a three-week trip, three years later, in 2011.

I wanted to forget her birthday. To spend the day in a fog and let it pass by me without so much as an acknowledgement. I wanted to celebrate her and forget about her in the same breath—anything to make the pain stay away for at least a day. For at least *that* day. Instead, the booze caused me to cry more easily and feel more deeply.

I tried to use alcohol to keep the grief at bay, to numb my feelings and memories. I wanted to hurt less, so I hurt myself more. Cabernet Sauvignon was chosen over prayer. I had walked through fire for the past eighteen months, and I didn't want to burn anymore. However, instead of being a salve, the booze was an accelerant. Emotions I hadn't known I had rose to the surface. I felt deeper, and it hurt.

The next special day on the calendar was Mother's Day. This was a holiday that was never celebrated in my house growing up, not even with breakfast in bed. Mom rarely wanted to be recognized, and because the day was always a Sunday, we always had a sporting event and church to go to. The first Mother's Day without Mom also happened to be my first Mother's Day with a mother-in-law. I had lost my first mother and gained my second.

Unfortunately, I wasn't able to see it so positively on that day. Instead of celebrating the amazing woman my mother-in-law is, I began the comparison game. I compared every aspect of Emily and Bonnie, grieving what I lost instead of celebrating what I still had. I put Mom on a pedestal, elevating the good things about her while willfully ignoring her flaws. In my head, I created a competition between two best friends and skewed it in such a way that only the dead one could win.

It took years for me to stop doing this. I was jealous that Bonnie was still here, and that Adam still had his mom to turn to. I was resentful that Bonnie was so loving, so tender, and so giving of everything she had because it made my loss seem that much greater. The more that I recognized how wonderful Bonnie was, the bigger the hole of Mom's death became. But how could I hold so much against a woman who was simply being who she was—a wonderful mother? It wasn't fair, and I knew it.

Bonnie, to her everlasting credit, was always ready to forgive when I came back for hugs in her kitchen, tearfully admitting that it was me who was pushing her away, not the other way around. As much as I tried to run from her love and her generosity, she never left, and she never gave up on me. It took a few years and a number of counselling sessions, but I can now confidently call her "Mom," and not my mother-in-law. She more than deserves that title.

The last of the firsts was Mom's death-aversary: July 31. On that day, I re-learned a new lesson: grief can be physically paralyzing. I took the day off of work and, at Adam's brilliant suggestion, had planned a day that would be a combination of remembering, self-care, and relaxing. It started with a favourite walk of Mom's through the woods, hammock in hand. One kilometre or so into the walk, I trudged into the thick forest, hung up my hammock, and crawled in. The double hammock cocooned me, and as I stared up at the leaves moving ever so slightly, I began to feel peace. The light flickering through the green would catch my eye, and I'd think that, for a moment, maybe God was giving me a sign. Everywhere, I looked for signs. Signs that Mom was coming back, or that I was going to be okay. Not getting anything that I would consider a sign—and I look for neon signs when it comes to God—I wandered back to the car and drove to Fort Langley and the cemetery.

I'd packed a blanket to sit on and brought Mom's regular Starbucks order, one for each of us, even though I knew her headstone would not be thirsty. I tried to have a conversation with Mom, and it was rather one-sided. Even as I longed to hear her voice, nothing would come. So I sat there, wondering. I wondered why Mom had to die. What was she doing in heaven? Did she miss me?

There are just so many unanswered questions. Why questions, and what-if questions. So in the absence of an answer or fact, you wonder. Dream. Imagine. Then you can make something happen in your mind that you can't in the real world.

Grief is a series of wonderings. You wonder about the things you did before your loved one died. You wonder about the things after. Philosophical and existential questions are asked, fully knowing you'll never get the answers. You pray to your loved one, hoping they will answer, instead of praying to God, who actually can. Faith and your reason for existence are questioned. Is God who you always knew Him to be?

God promised much in the Bible. He promised eternal life in heaven, with Him, for those who believe that Jesus died for them. He promised us Him: His presence and His peace when we fix our thoughts on what is true, pure, and just. He promised to never leave us or forsake us. He promised to make all things new, to make beauty from ashes. He didn't guarantee riches or a long life here on earth. As much as I wish I could say that I clung to these promises, I didn't. These promises felt far away in my time of grief, yet they remain unchanged. My brain was too full to remember them, and my eyes too moist to see that God and His promises are faithful, even when we are struggling to be.

As I sat on the sun-covered grass at Mom's grave, I began to openly weep, curse, and physically lay down next to the plot. I vaguely knew people were walking by, staring, and pointing at the woman having a crisis in a cemetery. No matter what I did, I couldn't leave. I couldn't walk away. It was as if our feet were tied together, hers six feet under. Walking away felt like I would be abandoning her when it truly felt like she had abandoned me.

In the end, it came down to a choice, and I could hear Mom's voice in my head with her common retort to my whines: "Do you have a piano tied to your ass?" So I removed said metaphorical piano and took a step. I took a step toward my car, and also a step toward healing.

It sounds cheesy, but it is the truth. The decision to stand up and walk away from Mom's grave took an unnerving amount of courage. But as I sat there, I began to think, *Haven't the last twelve months taught me anything?* I am capable. I am strong. I've walked through hardship, and this is just another one. God gave me every tool I needed to get through these tragedies and to make the hard and brave choices. I had to trust that He'd given me what I needed to walk away from her grave too, and that He would give me what I needed to heal. God is faithful to keep his promises, even when we lack the faith to believe them.

For two years, I continued to grieve and continued to heal.

Then one day, about two years after that fateful July day, I decided that it was time to clean out Mom's closet. The task had been on my mind for months, but I always found reasons to push it back: Dad's not ready. It's close to Christmas. I don't have time. But as I ran out of excuses, I called the only person I could imagine doing this unenviable task with, my best friend doctor turned family photographer at the hospital, Katie.

The day wasn't overly sad and, frankly, it was good to laugh with Katie, Cheryl, and other friends who joined us that day. We pulled out pair after pair after pair of shoes. There were so many shoes that I lined the hallway from Mom's room to mine, two pairs of shoes deep on either side of the hallway. It was about seventy-two pairs in total. From old pumps to gorgeous heels and a stunning pair of Prada stilettos, there was finally nothing left in the closet. Everyone there that day managed to find something of Mom's that fit to take home with them. Then it was on to the clothes. It seemed like the closet never ended, perhaps leading to Narnia whenever we would find the back. There was classy business attire and sequined dresses from the 90s. There were scarves upon scarves and an entire bin full of belts. Sweaters from Australia. Dresses from her kids' weddings. We chose, sorted, and folded clothes for ourselves, the donation centre, and the consignment store. We spent five hours unpacking her life to give it away to others. After closing up the suitcase that held all my newfound treasures from her closet, I cried. I was sad. Mom missed this bonding time. Her coveted clothes were now mine. These threads felt like all that was left of her.

As I looked that night at her sweaters and suits, now neatly hung up in my own closet, the reality that she wasn't coming home began to hit again. She couldn't come home. I couldn't pretend that she was on a business trip or in Hawaii. Mom never let me borrow her things—perhaps some accessories for an evening or a pair of pantyhose when I needed them for work, but never anything more than that. Likely, she didn't want me to ruin them. So seeing the clothes I had once asked to borrow hanging in my closet felt surreal.

In a way, I felt like I had violated Mom. I felt like I dug into her deepest secrets and broadcast them to the world. Or more like I'd amputated her, piece by piece, with each dress I took from her closet. In the lowest of thoughts, I felt like I was completely dismantling her, disrespecting her memory. These were the last physical reminders of her, things that I could touch and smell that were completely her.

* * *

Several years after Mom died, my dear friend Jodi sent me a poignant text message. She had lost her dad to a heart attack a few years before Mom died and knew the feeling of grief all too well. Her message captured what life after the death of a parent is like:

> *Neither of us dreamed of being in this Dead Parents Club, but it's been "nice" (what other word works?) to have someone in there who knew my dad. And hopefully you feel the same way as I do about your mom. You've led your life with grace and true grace for all of what you've been through.*

The Dead Parents Club was the most accurate thing I'd heard in a long time. It is a club that no one chooses to be a part of, but once you are in it, you never get to leave. Nor can you, should you want to. In this club are people who understand, who commiserate. These are the people you can vent to, cry with, and ask your dumb questions of. They are the people who check in on the hard days and who never need a response back. My personal Dead Parents Club is getting too full of members, which is heartbreaking in and of itself.

So in the hope that you never need to join my Dead Parents Club, or if you are helping those who have joined it, I want to give you a brief snapshot of some of the lessons about navigating grief that I've learned since joining this group:

1. Silence isn't awkward

It's a tweak of that old saying, but if you don't know what to say, don't say anything at all. Be with us, tell us you are here, and let it be at that. Tell that you are here and that you don't expect a response; give us the freedom to come to you when we can and when we are ready.

2. Check your words

If you start a sentence with "just" or "at least," we will tune out everything you say after that. Please don't minimize our experience with a comparison. No one has it worse than another. It all sucks. Instead, try "That is so hard" and see what happens.

3. Expect nothing

We all grieve differently, have our own timelines, and really don't know what to expect day in and day out. Keep your expectations of us low. Make space for us to talk about our loved ones, and you can use their names, or ask us questions. We do want to talk about them, so try to leave space for us to.

4. Platitudes and positivity only go so far

No, not everything happens for a reason, and no, it isn't all going to be okay. This is the worst thing we have been through. Try telling us that you are grateful for anything we want to share and mean it. Sometimes, we can't move on—and that's okay.

5. We love you. We aren't ignoring you.

Sometimes we get asked impossible questions, like "How are you really doing?" We don't know, we can't articulate it, or we simply don't want to tell you. Please don't take our silence personally. Just know that we might not have the energy, or words, to tell you what you are looking for. And, perhaps, we are trying to protect you from our burdens weighing as heavily on you as they do on us. They are so much for us to bear, we don't want to pass that on.

And if you really want to be practical, take care of the people we take care of. Take our kids for an evening, or ideally, a sleepover. Drop off food for dinner and breakfast the next day, schedule house cleaning, gift us small things that encourage us to take a break, because life goes on, even if we don't want it to.

That's why there can never be a new normal: because life goes on. It doesn't stop and then start again, unless you are the one being resurrected in heaven. Life continues, but it is never the same as it once was. So maybe it's not a new normal, it's just life? Normal is relative, after all.

016: A MOTHERLESS MOTHER

We got pregnant in September 2017, about two years after Mom passed away. I was working in corporate strategy at a local financial institution, and Adam was still progressing as a public practice accountant. We had been trying for a short while and, just before Adam went to Osoyoos with his parents, I took a test at our townhouse. With two very faint pink lines, Adam didn't believe it was positive. He's a man that needs concrete facts, and if the lines weren't almost red instead of pink, he wouldn't believe it. With that, he went on his merry way to a weekend at the cottage. That night, I went to Jayme's house in Vancouver and, on a whim, we went to Shoppers Drug Mart and picked up a pregnancy test. One with words to tell me if I was pregnant, instead of hard-to-interpret lines.

I peed on the stick but kept it hidden under the instructional sheet until Jayme could come in and read it for me. My heart was racing, and I could hear the heartbeat in my ears when she started crying, looked at me, and said, "You're having a baby."

In that instant, I became a mother. A motherless mother. While my heart soared for what my world would look like over the next few months, I instantly recognized that one of the main people you are supposed to share this secret with was absent.

Adam and Jayme did their best to make sure they fully filled that void. In those early weeks, Adam tempered his expectations to make sure I had all the naps I needed. Jayme checked in regularly to make sure that I was feeling okay, and to give me all the pregnancy and birth-related advice that she could. Without those two, those first weeks of secret keeping would have been extremely difficult to navigate by myself.

For all my friends who had been pregnant, their mothers played pivotal roles in their pregnancy. They were the ones who were told first, who gave advice on what to do for exhaustion, and who shared the family history with the doctor. I didn't have that. Their mothers were the ones to bring over dinner on the tough nights and go maternity clothes shopping with them, and I felt lost without that.

So others stepped in, in amazing ways. Friends took us to Buy Buy Baby to show us what we needed, and what baby items were gimmicks. Cody and Carlee threw us a shower from a few provinces away so that we could feel all the love from our family. Friends from my Bible study put together a "care for your vagina" package with all the things I didn't know I'd need postpartum. The stuff you don't want to buy, like stool softeners and pads thicker than my duvet. Friends threw more showers, Bonnie took me maternity dress shopping, and aunts prayed daily. My in-laws all helped paint and ready the nursery. Other friends leaned in more deeply with Dad, taking him to appointments when they conflicted with my own.

Time flew, and before we knew it and on his due date, our son Knox made his way into our world, with his father by my side and Jayme at my legs. Both there since the second we knew Knox was alive. He'd been a part of our hearts for nine months, and now he was in our arms. He was perfect, with a very big, bald head, a loud cry, and arms and legs that flew everywhere. Wrapped tight and snuggled, he was a dream. His eyes were bigger than his stomach: he regularly ate so much that he spat up more than even a hand towel could handle. Our world fit in an eight-pound vessel.

We called our families to join us at the hospital, not telling them the gender of our baby, just that there was a grandchild waiting to meet them. Based on how fast my in-laws arrived at the hospital, I think they had already left Abbotsford when we called. Kurt and Bonnie arrived, and both began tearing up as they met their first grandson. They held him, snuggled him, and kissed his face. Joelle and Robby, Adam's sister and brother-in-law, did the same. This little boy was bringing them as much joy as he brought to us. It was exactly as we'd pictured these meetings.

Cheryl brought Dad a few minutes later. He too started crying as he walked in and held his grandson.

"His name is Knox Mitchell," I said softly. His middle name, a nod to my brother's own.

"Oh. That's perfect," said Dad as he repeated Knox's name again and again under his breath.

He held Knox gently, patting his bum and kissing his brow. As he stared into Knox's eyes, he asked, "What's his name again?" It was a question without embarrassment and without worry. It was simply a grandfather wanting to make sure he honoured his grandson by calling him the right name.

This was not what I had pictured. But it was beautiful. I had this vision in my head of having a baby and my parents being the first ones to my side, knowing exactly what to do and what to say. I pictured them being in the hospital with us all night, holding the baby so Adam and I could sleep. Their phones were going to be full of pictures and constantly ringing with calls from their families congratulating them. None of this happened, but it was beautiful in its own way.

We made it home and the sleepless nights began. The difficult days came when Knox would cry and I couldn't figure out why, or make it stop. My thoughts began to wander, and my familiar friend grief showed up again. I wished my mom was there: she would have taken Knox at night, she would have taught me how to breastfeed, she would have made meals so I could snuggle my baby. I created this image in my head of Emily, the grandma. A title she would never bear on earth.

And therein lies the problem. I created this false narrative, this false image of who Emily the grandma would have been. I again put her on a pedestal and gave her all the grandmotherly qualities I had hoped and believed she would have. In reality, she may not have been any of those things. Or maybe she would; I'll never know. In my head, I created a legacy that never existed.

I had a close friend tell me that she couldn't imagine going through raising children without her mother. She meant this in a kind, "I can't believe you have to do this" way. And she is completely right. It is anything but easy to raise kids without your own mom to help you. Without someone close who has done it before, who knows you so well that they can predict your triggers. Without that person you can call on day or night to come and help, or listen, or just bring coffee in the morning. I didn't choose this—I didn't choose to move away from my mom or have an estranged relationship. Death separated us, and separated her from her grandkids. It feels vastly unfair.

Being a mom is anything but easy. I thought parenting one child was difficult and got angry whenever someone told me how easy I had it with just Knox. How could they know that I was up all night feeding by spoon because Knox wouldn't latch? It's not easy when you have a child who won't go more than two steps from me because he is anxious and wants to reattach his umbilical cord. It's not easy when you desire a high-level corporate career with a baby who won't give you any space beyond the car road mat on the floor and you.

So as the challenges mounted with Knox, I got sad and angry. I was diagnosed with postpartum depression, and I wished with all my might that Mom was here. At night, after I finally got him to sleep, I'd lay my head on my pillow, and my brain would scream out her name again. "Mom!" It was desperate. A longing cry for anyone to have answers, for her to save me from the hell that was no sleep. For her to hold my hand like when I was little, and to let her have control over the things I couldn't. The control that she excelled in, that excited her.

* * *

When I was pregnant with Knox, I was sure that I was having a boy but hopeful that I would have a girl. I wanted a little human to be named after Mom and to have a chance to build that quintessential mother-daughter relationship with. Instead, I got more than I could have imagined. In Knox, I got a little man who is so gentle, big-hearted, and sensitive. A boy who gets excited about everything and hugs unashamedly. He loves big. God knew I needed Knox to mold me, to soften me, and to introduce me to what it means to be a mother.

Knox was the one to remind me to be patient. He was my introduction to sleep deprivation, gracious in the days when I could barely function after no sleep. God gave me Knox, the exact child I needed, for the mother that He was preparing me to be.

So when I was almost ready to deliver our second baby in 2020, I was ready. This child was a breech baby, and at thirty-seven weeks, Adam and I went into the hospital for an external cephalic version: a procedure used to help turn the baby in your womb. While I lay on a bed in triage, the nurse hooked me up to a fetal heart monitor and got the ultrasound machine ready. The doctor made his way in and gave me warning. His eyes, behind his medical-grade mask, were kind. His words direct but compassionate.

"This is an extremely painful procedure, and you are going to need to breathe and relax as much as you can through it. It's not likely to be successful, and we have an operating room ready in case it is too much for the baby to handle. I'll try it twice only, and I can give you pain medicine after the first try if it is too much for you. I'll try turning the baby and we will check it with the ultrasound to make sure it is handling the procedure well before we try again."

With that, he rubbed ultrasound gel all over my extremely round stomach and began pushing down. He pushed down so hard and far that you could see the visible outline of the baby rather than a pregnant belly. Adam told me after that he could see the head and bum clearly, that was how hard the pressure was.

The doctor grabbed the baby's head and bum and slowly began to turn it. The pain was excruciating, feeling like my stomach was being flipped inside out and that every part of my womb was being ripped from its original place. He struggled to move the baby more than a few centimetres and checked its position with the ultrasound.

"The baby is tolerating it and you are too. I'm impressed. Can we try again? Do you need pain meds?" he asked.

"I'm fine. Just go again."

And so he did. Five more times. After six tries, the baby still wouldn't turn, and it was beginning to be too much for any of us to bear. I began sobbing, my face hidden in Adam's shoulder. "I'm so sorry," I whispered to him. "I'm so sorry I couldn't do this."

"Oh, Rayel," he said softly as he stoked my hair, "you are strong, and it will be fine. It's okay. I'm not mad. I am so proud of you."

The doctor grabbed my hand with both of his and looked me deep in the eye. "I've never seen anyone handle that like you did. You have nothing to be ashamed of, and you are not a failure. This baby is going to be strong like its mama, and you are going to be okay."

And with that one statement, my soul ripped open a little bit more. This baby was going to be strong, like me and like my mother before me. Even if all else was incompatible, there would be this similarity: strength. And as we would soon find out, strength was something this baby had in spades.

After the unsuccessful ECV, I started to wonder whether or not our baby's resistance to turn from breech position was an indication of what would come with their growing up. My anxiety was at an all-time high. I started to believe that this meant the baby and I would have a lifetime of clashing, of not being on the same page. Would we ever be compatible? If we couldn't get along in utero, what would it be like later? I began to emotionally disconnect myself from the baby, thinking that this would protect me from a future of chaos and conflict with them. Emotions were guiding everything, and my psychiatrist assigned by the hospital was worried especially about the dissociation.

I thought I was being totally rational. If we couldn't even coalesce when the baby had no opinions, voice, or authority, it was going to be terrible once it was outside. We were already off on the wrong foot.

In hindsight, these were all signs of prenatal anxiety and markers for postpartum depression. Thankfully, I had an Ob-Gyn, registered clinical counsellor, and psychiatrist who also all saw these markers and started treatment immediately. I'd like to tell you that it was all solved once the baby was born and in my arms, but that would be a lie.

But when Savannah Emily was born by C-section on a cold Wednesday afternoon in December, there was absolutely nothing going on in my head except that I had a daughter. When Adam looked over the curtain to tell me that we had a girl, I didn't believe him. She was healthy, she was loud, and she loved being cuddled. As she started her life, she immediately took to nursing and loved to sleep on my chest: all things I had assumed wouldn't happen because we would be so incompatible.

At the time I'm writing this, Savvy is eighteen months old, and here is what I know. She is a little girl who knows what she wants and will work hard to get it. Whether it's crawling over cushions to reach my coffee cup or stealing toys from her brother, she will do what she wants. She is not overly affectionate but will give us hugs and kisses when we ask for it. She is busy and will not sit still for anything or anybody. In short, she is just like her grandma.

As she continues to grow, I see more and more of Mom in her. Heaven help the person who tries to take Savvy's pretend purse from her, or tell her that she can't do something. She will move mountains to get what she wants, and is almost looking for a challenge to overcome. She drinks coffee from my cup. No milk and in large gulps. Mom would have been so proud of her granddaughter.

How is it possible that having a daughter brings me closer to my dead mother? Getting to raise a little girl is offering me a glimpse into what it was like for Mom to raise me. Raising Savvy is helping me understand what Mom worried about, and how she saw herself in me. How we mirrored each other. As much as I can see Mom in Savvy, I can see her in me and in the way that I react and interact with her. It's both freeing and terrifying.

We often say that we don't want to be like our moms, and that was certainly the case for me. I didn't want to be as ambitious as she was, as singularly focused as she was. But I am. The genes are strong and the blood runs thick between us. There are parts of her that I can't separate from even if I wanted to. But what I am also learning is that I have the strength and power to forge my own path, in motherhood and life. That I have the ability to stop generational sins and patterns, to create something new and lasting for my son and daughter. That I can choose the best of my heritage and use it just as intentionally as I choose to not use some elements of my heritage and genetics.

It takes work, though. Choosing to allow my children to fail, or to not be in control of things, is not easy. From day one as a mom, I've realized I can't control them. Try as I might, their sleep schedules are 100% their own. I can give them food but can't force them to eat it. It's going to take prayer to let go of the bigger things, the stuff I want to hold on to. That I've deemed necessary for their protection.

Because if I've learned anything over the last few years, I can't protect everyone from everything.

These "shoulda" moments continued after Savannah was born and my life as a mom of two began to settle. In her first three months, Savvy liked to be awake and party from 2:00 a.m. to 4:00 a.m., almost every night. She wasn't upset, she wasn't even happy, she was just awake. So she and I would sneak downstairs to the couch, turn on the TV, and watch some volleyball or *Gilmore Girls* until we'd both fall asleep there. Her head on my chest and her breath warming my neck soon became the only way either of us could sleep. But the next morning, there was no rest to be had. Knox would be up, ready to play, and despite only getting four or five hours of sleep total, most of that on the couch, mom duties prevailed.

It was those mornings that I would have given anything for Mom to be here. She was the one that I wanted to call, the one that I should have called for rescue. She was the one person that I wouldn't have felt guilty calling. As absolutely wonderful as Bonnie, Cheryl, and Roxie were, I believed there had to be a limit to their graciousness, to their giving. I was tapped out, so they must have a limit too. I couldn't ask *again* for their babysitting or bother them *again* for meals. My world was of my own making, one where I was extremely independent, and that also meant very alone. As hard as these women, and my friends, tried to break in, I kept them at bay. I believed that I could do it on my own.

And what's worse? I believed God wanted me to do it on my own. Why else would He have allowed Mom to be taken away from me? I thought that I had to do it on my own, that it was His will.

In the days after Mom died, my cousin told me something that I'll never forget. He said, "Rayel, people say that the Bible tells us that you will only be given what you can handle. That's not totally true. You are sometimes given more than you can handle, and that's exactly where and when you need to rely on God."

And sometimes, God gives you a village. He gives you people who love you, whom He put in your life years and years ago for a time like this. He gives you strength and resilience through their acts of service and kindness.

This is still a lesson that I am learning, one that I will probably always be working through. I am learning to ask for help when I need it and that asking for help is not a sign of weakness but a sign of courage and self-awareness. But this is also a generational habit that I want to break. I want my kids to know they can and should ask for help, because life is a team sport, one we cannot play alone. I want them to see that in our family, we are grateful to say yes to help more than we say no. God did not intend for us to do life alone. I am blessed to have people in my circle who will stick with me, even when I try and step out on my own.

In the beginning, being a motherless mother felt terrifying and lonely. It felt guilt-ridden and expectation-laden. Instead, what it is turning into is a world full of freedom. While Mom "should have" been here and "could have" been the best grandma, I am going to raise these kids to know her, to know God, and to know their own strength, because that is one genetic trait that will live on.

017: A DEPENDENT DAD

Backing up, at twenty-six years old, my dad became my dependent. His appointments became our appointments, his errands became our errands. Lawyers, doctors, and wealth managers no longer handled just Dad's affairs, but the entire family's. He lost privacy, but we called it "caregiving." And it wasn't just his privacy, but ours too. Detailed reports about his health were sent to family and friends over text: "Dad's experiencing some weird breathing patterns and having a hard time sleeping at night. The doctors think it's just natural given where he's at, but he won't do a sleep apnea test. So we are going to just monitor it. Thanks for praying!"

His well-being was a shared goal among many. Every one of us wanted him to be happy, healthy, and looked after, and that often meant sacrifices on our end. A sacrifice of time. Or sometimes, sweat. Often, tears.

With Dad, my first true test of "out of the hospital" caregiving came that night when his friends, Perry, Cheryl, Daryl, Janet, Adam, and I sat in our townhouse to make his schedule of care. The night that we divided up sleepovers and day trips to the grocery store. And it never stopped. Those people never stopped.

The tricky thing about caring for an adult is that they are still an adult. They still deserve independence, having always made their own decisions. They've earned our faith because they've proven to be trustworthy, even if it was years before. We think the best of them. Disciplining them is inconceivable. Maintaining their dignity is at the forefront of decisions.

It's different with a child. We expect and sometimes demand that toddlers listen to us. We have grace for their mistakes because they have never been in a particular situation before. They cheat, and we correct. They want independence. We give it in measured doses. Perhaps this is just my parenting style, but no matter yours, the way you'd treat a five-year-old child is likely markedly different from how you'd treat a sixty-year-old dependent. The tough conversations that you have a "right" to have with your child, you don't necessarily have that innate "right" to as an adult parenting your parent. With adults, it seems to be more negotiation, phrasing in a way that will help them (in their sometimes limited capacity) to see your point of view. And sometimes, you realize it's easier to ask for forgiveness than permission. You just do and pray that you can handle them hating you for a while for taking away something that matters to them.

So that's why, when my kids were born, taking care of Dad proved to be even more complex.

I'm not saying that Dad had the mental capacity of a five-year-old child. No, he was still wise in his own way. He could communicate, could problem solve to a limited extent. In general, he knew right from wrong. The filter that lives between our minds and our brain was non-existent for him, though, often resulting in words that could sting if the wrong person heard them.

"Rayel, there's no way that girl played volleyball. She's way too short!"

Sometimes, it was funny.

Other times, as you can imagine, embarrassing.

* * *

Any working parent knows that their schedule is full. In any one week, you have a dozen of your own meetings. Then add in a few things from the never-ending housework to-do list. Don't forget the swim lessons, or the soccer practice. There's homework to supervise, meals to prepare. Playdates, church obligations, volunteer opportunities that you signed up for a month ago that you are now regretting. Then, importantly, there are the doctors' appointments and the time suck that is a dentist appointment. Haircuts. Eyeglass appointments. Groceries to buy. There's Netflix to watch, dang it!

So imagine all of this and then adding another full-fledged adult's responsibilities to yours. The invisible workload is often forgotten. The worry and anxiousness, the planning and prep. It's never-ending and such a load to carry.

And then there were his doctors' appointments, which weren't just once a year but once or twice a month. At one point, Dad had regularly scheduled visits with a family doctor, cardiologist, psychiatrist, and the lab for blood work. Combining this with our family's schedule, something had to give.

That something was my pride. Again.

No matter how many times I was reminded that I couldn't do it all, my default was to believe that I could. That if I worked hard, I'd succeed. Everything could be handled with good planning and a high credit card limit. We weren't going to bother other people with our problems. We'd take care of them ourselves. Wasn't this what I'd done my entire life?

Often, it felt like a choice had to be made. My kids, or my father. How could I give them both the best of me without sacrificing the other? How could they both get the amazing life they deserved if I clung to the other? There was guilt no matter the decision. There was a constant pull on my time, on my emotions, and some days, whoever yelled the loudest got what they wanted. It was relentless, even when I tried to carefully prioritize everyone's needs: 1) The person who yells the loudest; 2) the person who is most at imminent risk of injury, illness, or death; 3) the person whose needs can be fixed quickly; and 4) people who have it worse off than me (which is everyone in my mind . . . despite it all, I feel lucky).

My time belonged to everybody else because I thought they deserved it. Perhaps it was a martyr mindset. Perhaps I thought too highly of myself and my contribution to the world. *What if I let them do it alone? What if I said no instead of yes? Maybe I should take that bath I promised myself four months ago?* Anytime I'd get burned out, I had to ask for help. I had no choice if I wanted to physically breathe. I'd keep going through cycles of trying to do it all, burning out, resting, trying to do it all, burning out, resting . . . I'm nothing if not hard-headed and stubborn.

Pride diminished, I would send a text like, "I don't know how to do this. Can you help?" And anyone on the receiving end always responded with "Yes."

In one instance, it was a family wedding. Our cousin, Dad's niece Laura, was getting married in Alberta. Dad had a special fondness for Laura, often texting her on weekends to wish her well. To say that he adored her would be an understatement.

"Rayel," he began one day, "I'll just drive to Alberta for the wedding. I don't need help."

My eyes visibly rolled to the back of my head. Shoulders rose for both of us, in anticipation of a battle as I prepared my usual response to Dad's belief that he was capable of what he had been eight years ago.

"Dad, that's impossible. You have a hard time driving twenty kilometres away without getting confused. I can't let you drive all the way to Alberta. It's not safe, and I'd be worried about you the entire way."

He nodded reluctantly. Recognizing his new reality was not easy, and rarely positive. We would have this conversation often, and each time, at the end, he would sigh and return to the single-draw solitaire on his iPad, eyes downcast and shoulders resigned.

Setting boundaries for Dad, for the purposes of his safety, was difficult. To maintain and to enforce. He was an adult. No adult likes being told no or having their freedom restricted. You dream of independence when you are a kid. To have it abruptly taken away from you at fifty-six was a less-than-ideal outcome. It was out of his control and inadvertently put me into the proverbial driver's seat.

It meant that, as his caregiver, I made every decision with his safety in mind. The mental math of balancing his perceived limitations with his desires was endless. Where I felt concessions could be made one day were vastly different the next. Some days I was completely fine with him distributing financial gifts to charities, and the next, I felt I had to rein him in. His limits were fluid, running with my emotional state. My stress was not good for his leash length.

It left him, and those around him, confused. Why could Rayel unilaterally determine something was acceptable today but not tomorrow? And worst of all, I imagine them saying, "Why can't she tell us why?" I picture their anger toward me because of it, and it haunts me. I want to please everyone and hurt no one.

The logic behind it is indescribable. Feelings guided my decisions. Logic and long-term thinking were often put aside. Adam learned to roll with it. For a man full of logic, he began to accept "I'm not sure why, but that's what I'm doing," as validation for my choices. He trusted me. Dad trusted me.

Wrong choices were made. In the name of his safety, I crippled him. I stunted his recovery. All I could do was justify it to myself and stand up to do it all over again. If he couldn't learn to fail, could he get better? We learn from mistakes, and I wasn't allowing him to make any. I wasn't letting him stretch. Maybe if I had let him drive to Calgary, he'd feel more comfortable driving to our house now. By not even letting him TRY, I think I was stunting his confidence in his ability and recovery.

During one Thursday night session, full of Kleenex and running mascara, my counsellor, Tracey, offered this perspective.

"What if, instead of asking what's best for your dad when you make a choice, what if you ask, what's the most loving choice?"

My brain turned inside out. *What if I made the most loving choice? Isn't that what I'd been doing all along?*

No, it wasn't. If I was honest with myself, I was making the safe choice. What I thought was the best decision. The most loving choice, in some cases, was to let Dad fail. Or letting him do what he wanted. It meant he had made his own mind up about something. Restoring his freedoms, respecting his abilities and desires. Maybe love meant more than security.

With that in mind, I wanted to make the most loving choice for Dad. I wanted him to be able to go to Laura's wedding. Desire and reality are still different. My childcare constraints and personal capacity hadn't changed. My weariness was heavy. But my brother noticed and stepped in.

The logistics were complex. Cody would fly from Winnipeg to Calgary and wait for Dad at the airport. He'd get a rental car and hotel, playing chauffeur to wherever Dad needed to go for the weekend. He would be the pill pusher, making sure Dad took his meds on time. He would take care of it all, balancing his own visits with his friends in Calgary around Dad's schedule.

My only job was to get Dad on the plane. At Canadian airports, you can ask for a gate pass at a check-in desk to help family or children get to, or on, the airplane. It's a special ticket that buys you a pat down at security but no uncomfortable seat on the plane. This ticket was gold, and it was free. With this ticket in my hand, Dad's fidgeting slowed. His breathing calmed, and his walk became slower, more confident. His hands tightly gripped his backpack, his jacket full of coins that were quickly laid on the security conveyer belt. But he was doing it, and he knew he could.

Plus, with Dad having a memory impairment, the airline was willing to put a "tag" on the manifest that indicated so. If he dozed on the plane and woke up wondering where he was, the flight attendants had a script. "Mr. Quiring, you are on your way to Calgary for a wedding." It was a structure that set him up for success. He could do this.

And he did. He slightly nervously got on the plane and smartly followed the baggage claim signs when he landed in Calgary. And there, waiting at the bottom of the stairs, was his son. His son, who was ready with a huge hug, and who would continue to set Dad up for success throughout the weekend. Cody made the weekend possible, giving Dad new core memories that he would talk about, repeatedly, for the weeks and months to come.

It's a fine balance, knowing where to draw the line. Where to let Dad fly, and where to let him fall. What's the best choice?

The secret is that there is no best. Nothing about this is ideal. Every decision comes with risk, with trade-offs. And what makes sense to you may not to the people around you, and justifying your decision might only make the rationale more grey and confusing. But what cannot be disputed is when you make the most loving decision for someone. Those decisions rarely look logical. They often signal surrender. Of yourself, of your ability to control. They focus the decision on what's possible, on the recipient rather than yourself. Those are the decisions that are easier to live with. No questions asked.

Before and after that Calgary trip, Cody had always been in contact with Dad, calling him daily to check in on how he was feeling ("fine") or what he was up to ("sitting on the couch this way, and then that way"). No matter how routine the conversations, Cody would call. Dad looked forward to it, and couldn't remember that each call was like Groundhog Day, the same as the day before. As I got over-whelmed and exhausted caring for the kids and Dad, Cody stepped in even deeper. He would send dad jokes and memes. He'd continue to call and FaceTime, and he'd come back to BC from Winnipeg as often as he could.

Repeating the same conversation over and over again is exhaust-ing. I couldn't do it anymore. I wanted a break; I wanted rest. So Cody gave me that. He took on the load of talking to our dad, and he did it with love for Dad and I, not out of obligation. He sacrificially gave his time to make his father's day, taking an unimaginably big load off of my shoulders.

* * *

Inevitably, there were appointments that I couldn't make. Conflicts that couldn't be avoided. Like clockwork, Dad's 8:00 a.m. cardiolo-gist appointment always ran into daycare drop off or an executive presentation that I had to give. No matter what, I was running into something. And we'd have to book cardiologist appointments four to six months in advance because there just aren't enough appointments. Inevitably, work would add in last-minute meetings or presentations that I hadn't foreseen so much earlier. It was always something differ-ent, but the commonality was that it was always during work hours.

With joy, Adam took Dad to these appointments when I couldn't. He'd listen to the doctors closely and report back to our group chat with Cody and Carlee all the details. Adam would take Dad for coffee, talking about the mundane things and, given they were both dads, sharing dad jokes at every opportunity. He became my father's safe place. Being the son-in-law, Adam never had to ask Dad how he was doing. He never had to check in on Dad's bowel movements or blood pressure. And Dad seemed to appreciate that; Adam became his place to escape and where he didn't have to worry about his body, or his mind. Adam accepted him just as he was.

Every other month, Adam would take Dad to see the barber, who also happened to be our close friend, Scott. The event would always begin with a reminder text from Adam in the afternoon,

"Rod, I'm coming to get you at 6:15 for our haircuts with Scott. I'll see you soon!"

After the scheduled pick-up, the two would take the short fifteen-minute drive from Dad's apartment to Cloverdale, chatting the entire way. At one particular intersection, Dad always made the same comment on each trip: "I engineered that building." He didn't.

Passing a farm on the drive, Dad always noticed the same thing. Similarly, a repeat statement came from his lips as they drove past a landmark.

"That's where the Ride to Conquer Cancer starts." He was right.

No matter the repetition, Adam continued to take Dad every eight weeks on a Monday to see Scott. The drive was routine. The haircut? Exactly the same every time. Scott and Adam would hear the same jokes from Dad, the same laughter. There was beauty in the mundane. Dad wasn't changing.

* * *

Regardless of who took Dad where, we still had two kids. Two littles who needed to nap and be fed, and generally, a *Good Housekeeping* magazine at the doctor's office could not entertain them. On the rare occasion that they did accompany Dad to an appointment, Dad was more thrilled than anybody. He'd snuggle them in the waiting room, quietly tickling their toes. They would scream, and he would chuckle. Nothing fazed him, and when his grandkids were on his knee, there was no sense that anything else existed in the world. He loved them deeply and fully.

During most of those appointments, family watched the kids. Or "chosen family," as we called some of them. Cheryl, my mom's close friend, was Nana to the kids. Not only would she watch them regularly during the week while I worked, but she would pick up extra shifts with them so Adam and I could attend Bible study, go on a date, or, in this case, take Dad to the doctor. She never minded. Blood may not have connected her to Knox and Savannah, but her heart did. She was their Nana. Her hugs were wide for them, and her kisses stopped their tears. They loved her.

Roxie was another of our family friends, an aunt by choice. She and her husband, Orv, were our last-minute regulars who lived all of five minutes down the road. Grandma and Grandpa Harder, as they would be called, were superheroes. Already grandparents of their own seven grandkids, including two sets of twins, they took ours on without looking back. Their house literally had an unlocked door, and Knox learned early to walk on in and make himself at home, just like we all did. They were home to us. There was always food, always conversation. Their warmth was felt through laughs. Whenever a last-minute appointment for Dad came up, or an unexpected need, they showed up. They always showed up.

And for those that weren't looking after my kids, they were looking after us. On more than a few occasions, Perry, who was Cheryl's husband, would take Dad for coffee. They'd laugh too loud, have too much fun. They focused on the present, not the past or the future. Conversation swirled around kids and grandkids. Sometimes they'd go together to the doctor with Perry, an accountant by trade, providing detailed notes like this immediately after.

"They said his blood pressure was 110 over 80 and his next step is to visit the family doctor for an update in medications. The nurse was optimistic, but the doctor was hesitant."

And then I would relay that message to Daryl, another chosen uncle who, as a paramedic, would translate these medical terms that were presented with accountant precision back to me to understand. "He's going to be okay," was the common translation that Daryl would present. Daryl and Janet, who had moved to Kelowna since Dad's stroke, would regularly check in on us and Dad. While not as present in the day-to-day, they made their love felt in other ways. Short texts, remembrances of special days, and hugs tighter than my pants after Christmas dinner.

It doesn't only take a village to raise a child—it takes a village to care for an adult. And I don't just mean Dad. I mean me.

Dad's ongoing care is only possible because of our team of people. Adam, Cody, and my sister-in-law, Carlee, are the core. But the close second is all these people. People who care for our kids so we can care for Dad. It's the little things. Friends who give Adam and I the night off so we can reconnect as a couple. It's the simple things, like an uncle who inspires me with a new hobby, coaching me in it and giving me a new focus. Family who recognize that we are in a tough season and bring over meals, or neighbours who do a Costco trip for us.

Villages can be big, they can be small. No matter their size, find yourself in it. Contribute to it when you can with your gifts and your abilities. Some seasons you'll be able to give lots. Other seasons, absolutely nothing. But hear me loud and hear me clear: you cannot do this alone.

Trust me, I've tried. Many, many times. You've seen me regularly fall into this prideful trap and barely come out the other side. Sometimes, I don't. But believe me when I say that life gets more full, and often easier if you let other people join you. It's worth laying down your pride and independence. It's worth trusting them and God for.

* * *

By 2018, when Knox was born, we started laying hints that maybe Dad should consider downsizing. He was living in the same 2,200-square-foot house that Cody and I had grown up in. Of those 2,200 square feet, he used approximately 300 of them: the living room, his bedroom, and the bathroom. The absence of the kitchen on that list is no oversight. Dad's menu consisted of grocery store sandwiches and takeout pizza, with the occasional barbequed burger thrown in.

Dad's lack of attention to detail and inability to initiate anything due to his brain injury meant that we started seeing wear and tear on the house that he previously would have been able to, and want to, fix. Sink drains were becoming clogged with leftover pizza toppings that he'd mistakenly dropped. Burned out light bulbs stayed unlit, partially because he didn't notice them and partially because he thought he had already changed them. His coffee table was littered with old papers and church bulletins. Dad didn't want to lose anything, so everything had to be in plain sight. His fear overtook his brain. The house was always warm, relatively clean, and tidy, but the little things were starting to slip.

Adam and I began to bring Knox over to snuggle with Grandpa so that we could do some maintenance. Adam would regularly change the burned out bulbs or clean up the yard while I would wash sheets and put garbage away. Dad would happily cuddle his grandson while sitcoms played in the background, *The Big Bang Theory* being a favourite of both Knox and him.

Cody and Carlee, childless at the time, made their own trip to BC in 2018, specifically to help Dad clean up his house in case he should decide to move quickly. The two of them spent almost two full days cleaning out Dad's garage. Tools purged, bins labelled. They found all kinds of treasures, like our old Disney VHS tapes, high school sports trophies, and some very embarrassing photos of my awkward years. They worked and sweat. Dust, dirt, and some small animal droppings were everywhere. They also dealt with Dad and his anxiety throughout. Dad hesitated to throw away anything, his mind asking, "What if I need it and don't know where it is?" about anything, from a hand saw to cross-country skis from the 1980s.

I can't imagine how hard that would be. To be so untrusting of your brain that you second guess everything. I experienced a small glimpse of that in early motherhood when the sleepless nights wreaked havoc on my memory. But it was fleeting. Nothing at all compared to the constant anxiety of wondering where you put your shoes, or if you left the stove on. And the emotional toll of worrying would be exhausting, creating a perpetual cycle. The more he worried, the more tired he became. And the more tired he was, the more he worried. It was never ending.

And there was little we could do to help. I'd occasionally get calls about where he left something, but the worry of missing an appointment meant Dad was often over thirty minutes early for it. Or, in one situation, Dad called me, certain that the world had changed.

"Rayel!" he shouted. "I took a nap and when I woke up, the sun was on the wrong side of the house!"

Confused, I responded, "What are you talking about?"

"When I went to sleep, it was eleven, and now it's six and the sun is on the west side of the house. It's morning. It's supposed to be on the east!" he answered anxiously. His words were quick and clipped.

"Dad, it's 6:00 p.m. The sun is on the west. Check the weather network on channel 18. It'll tell you the time."

His brain was constantly out to trick him, and his lack of sleep didn't help.

Dad was in no rush to move. His house was paid for, his needs met. But almost suddenly, in January 2019, Dad was ready for a change of scenery. He told us that he didn't want to be like his parents, holding on to their house until things were too late, making it hard on him. He wanted to make life easier for his children, so he was willing to give up his independence and way of living to make that happen. Now he tells his friends that he decided to move for me. That he could see that he was becoming too much of a burden for me and didn't want to do to me what his parents had done to him—by staying in their own place longer than they should have.

We went on a fact-finding mission, looking up independent living residences close by that met a certain set of criteria. It had to be in the neighbourhood he was currently in, walking distance to a coffee shop, have parking, and ideally have increased care options should he get worse. This extremely close set of criteria meant that one option was left. This home, luckily, had an apartment available for him within the next six months.

And just like that, we began the frenzy to pack up his house and get him moved into the next season of his life. It was a beautiful June weekend when Cody flew back, and all our friends came to the house to mark the transition with us. We knew it would be a busy day, but there was no way to prepare for the army of supporters that came to our side. We'd called on our family friends, but others, like Brad, Dad's one-time volleyball opponent now turned wealth manager, simply showed up. By 8:00 a.m., Kurt and Bonnie had taken Knox to their house for a sleepover so Adam and I could focus on the task at hand. We arrived at the house to a very anxious Dad and a brother who was ready to get to work.

We set a plan. Cody and I would move from room to room ahead of the others to set aside anything that we wanted to keep or not be thrown away. Then Adam would come behind us and direct things into a "dump" pile or a "donate" pile, both of which took up the driveway and front yard. Our friends would empty cabinets so we could look at what was in them, and once decisions were made on their fate, they would run them to the appropriate pile. Others would then load up trucks to make trips to Salvation Army or the dump. Anything that Cody and I weren't keeping was fair game. People took vases. Others, old toys. And others laid claim to furniture. Our chosen cousin, Shayne, became misty-eyed when we offered him the piano.

The piano was a fixture in our home. Other than the forced piano lessons that Cody and I took as kids, Christmas was the only time it made music. And only played by Mom. Her fingers would quickly float over the keys. She didn't need the green hymnal to know what notes to play. She was a regular pianist at her church as a teen. She knew the score from memory. Every Christmas she would play uplifting Christmas carols, singing quietly alongside while the rest of us went about our business. And when seasons in her life were particularly challenging, like when she lost her job in 2006, that hymnal would come out. Her voice would soften and her ears would tune to the untuned piano.

Shayne, like her, was a gifted pianist. I don't know if, in hindsight, I ever saw him use any sort of sheet music. His intuition guided him across the keys. When he and his family would come over for our annual Christmas dinner together, he would inevitably sit down and play so forcefully that the adults in the room would ask him to quiet down. This piano was his connection to my mom. He still keeps her alive through the music he plays on it, a tribute to their shared love of those ivory keys.

When we'd finished unloading the house, we'd made somewhere north of four trips to the dump and six trips to the Salvation Army. The collective sweat from the group could have filled a small bathtub. Our arms were tired, and so were our hearts.

Why is it hard to let go of things? They are just things—blankets, Christmas decorations, memorabilia. Despite their physical weight, they are heavy. Full of memories, of love. They carry our expectations, whether met or unmet. For Dad, these things were full of reminders of what was, of what should have been. Toys that were stored for twenty years for grandchildren were now being moved to the dump.

Rather than seeing what Dad gained by moving to a new apartment, all I could see was what he was losing. What he'd already lost.

It was another case of the "woulda, coulda, shoulda" moments. The things we subconsciously counted on let us down. Him being an active grandfather, downsizing to a condo first, growing old with Mom. It was too soon. While necessary, it felt premature simply because of his age.

We left the minimal amount of furniture in the house to stage it for the open houses that were upcoming. But now, we had the responsibility of selling the house that we grew up in. And given Dad's condition, I had to do it as a power of attorney.

The day before Mom went in for brain surgery, we recognized that both her and Dad's wills were not up-to-date, nor did they have a listed power of attorney. Given she was about to have her brain tickled by a neurosurgeon, we got a lawyer into the hospital to draft up her wishes as a just-in-case insurance plan. Same-day lawyers are well worth the money. We did Dad's at the same time, with Mom opting to list me as both of their designates because I lived here.

What I didn't realize is that this power of attorney document is both a barrier and a golden ticket. As Dad deferred his decisions to me, I used this blue-cornered document daily. It lived in my glove box. Not safe, but accessible. I found myself pulling out this document to talk on the phone with his insurance provider. It was my way in to make change for Dad's benefit. The bank wouldn't talk to me without seeing this piece of paper. I couldn't renew his car insurance without it on file. But once in, I could make anything happen. I became Dad, his designate and his imposter. Someone famous once said, "with great power, comes great responsibility," but when you're stewarding life for those you care about, it's a great responsibility that requires great power. This power of attorney became my super power.

So as it came time to sell the house, that blue-cornered paper made yet another appearance. When you are trying to sell a property that isn't your own, there are several additional hoops to jump through. It's all about risk mitigation. In no way did I want to be liable for not disclosing something that was wrong with the house. I knew some things, but not the entire story. Adam had made a herculean effort in maintaining a house that wasn't his own. But his efforts could not fix everything. Nor did he want to.

The day the house closed was bitter. We gathered my parents' friends for one final toast in the empty, echo-filled house that Cody and I grew up in. Perry and Cheryl, Orv and Roxie, Kurt and Bonnie, Dad, Adam, and I all showed up, with Cody, Daryl, and Janet joining by FaceTime. We slowly walked the house and recounted the meals we ate there together. We laughed at the stories of Catch Phrase games played in the family room, of piano music wafting from the living room, and of slamming doors upstairs to keep the boys out of the girls' room during Nerf gun battles. There were a lot of tears. It felt like the end of a really long chapter, one that had a wonderful beginning, a fantastic middle, and a really horrible ending. We toasted Mom, Dad, and all of our memories with limoncello. As everyone left, I did a final walk-through to turn out the lights.

The close of this season of our lives suddenly hit hard. I stood in the foyer of the house and began screaming, yelling for Mom.

"Mom!" I yelled. "Where are you? MOM!"

My words caught in my throat, my eyes blind with tears. Where was she? I was like a scared child, calling for her mom to come rescue her from a bad dream full of monsters and bad guys. But instead, cancer was the monster, and a stroke was the bad guy. She couldn't save me. She wasn't here. Dad seemed to need more help than I could give him. The walls echoed my yells but never provided a response. I was alone in a house that had always been full.

She should have been there, deciding if her Singer sewing machine should be thrown in the trash. Or dividing up her favourite wines among her favourite people. She should have been the one to hold

Dad's hand as they walked to a new chapter in independent living. Our family felt incomplete.

* * *

Every now and again, that power of attorney document wasn't enough. I couldn't sweet talk my way into getting something done on Dad's behalf. Often when on the phone with a service provider, they would need Dad to authorize talking to me because they couldn't physically see the delegation paperwork. And just as often, Dad wasn't physically around when I needed to talk to the service providers.

We lied. Every now and again when this happened, "Rod" would come to the phone and authorize the person on the other end to talk to me. "Rod" in many of these cases had a voice that sounded an awful lot like my husband. In fact, he was my husband. That seems weird to write! Adam, on occasion, would pretend to be my dad in order to authorize them to speak with me. If anyone is reading this who thinks this is wrong, please know that my dad always did want and need me to talk to these particular people, but he couldn't always be around for an hour while I waited on hold. So we found a way around it.

* * *

In 2020, the world stopped. COVID-19, a virus that changed the way the world works, accelerated its infection rate. At eleven months old, Knox knew the words pandemic and quarantine. Words that I, at thirty-one, had just recently come to understand. Dad was in his care facility, living relatively as normal. Until we got an email on March 22 from the residence that strongly encouraged Dad not to leave the building "for his safety and the safety of his fellow residents." Just five days later, on March 27, the spread of the virus confined all the home's residents, including Dad, to his four-hundred-square-foot apartment for what would become thirty-six days. His meals were delivered and his temperature monitored daily as COVID-19 ran rampant through the building.

While safe, he was bored. During that time, he gained about forty pounds, lost all muscle tone, and asked for an increase in his depression medication. At the end of the thirty-six days, we took him outside to play cars with Knox on the sidewalk, where we could still "distance." Dad squatted down to play with Knox and needed me to lift him back up as he had no balance and no muscle strength in his legs to stand from a squat.

So how do you support those in isolation? How do you care for those you can't physically help?

I took lessons from Cody and Carlee. They'd spent years living in Winnipeg, supporting Dad and us from afar. What would they do? We talked, a lot. We kids called Dad daily. The conversations were short and repetitive; no one was allowed to leave their homes or see anybody, so nothing new really happened.

"What'd you do today, Dad?"

"Nothing. Food came, watched some TV. How about you?" he would recite.

"Same old. Same old."

Dad's ability to do laundry was also restricted. We had him load up a suitcase with his dirty clothes, and a staff member took it from outside his suite door and left it outside for us to pick up. The process reversed once we'd washed and folded the clothes. Weekly, we'd bring bags of frozen food and treats from the grocery store to tide Dad over in between meals. The home-provided meals were meant for the appetites of people in their eighties, not a man of sixty-one years. He needed more than what was being delivered in the Styrofoam takeout boxes three times a day.

The year 2020 had the nicest spring in the Lower Mainland. Warm weather and clear skies were regularly appearing, making all the forced time at home just that much nicer. We had pulled Knox from daycare, fearful that he would catch the virus from another child, and we worked our days and meetings around his schedule. While one of us was on the phone, the other was watching Knox. Or taking him to visit Dad.

Dad was fortunate to have a balcony overlooking the parking lot. On the second floor, we could easily yell at each other. With one parent working, the other would watch Knox and take him to visit Grandpa. We'd set up camp on the sidewalk. We'd use chalk and play tic-tac-toe with Dad directing his moves from his balcony. The ground became littered with scratched out games. He and Knox would have races, Dad on his balcony and Knox on the sidewalk, each going as far as they could, as fast as they could. We'd toss chocolates up to him, snacking together despite being a floor apart. Dad was so happy to see us, always smiling and excited to interact with his grandson as best he could.

This time of isolation forced Adam and I to experience the smallest glimpse of what was likely going on for Cody and Carlee. How to worry about, and take care of, someone when you can't physically be with them. It required creativity and proved that proximity, while easier, did not impact strength of relationship. That with ingenuity and intention, the people you love can still feel cared for. Cody and Carlee had been doing this for years, and now it was our turn.

Surprisingly, this time reinforced the joy that can come with being in the middle of caring for everyone. It wasn't all bad. Yes, challenging. And yes, happy. The two coexisted in the delivery of treats, surprising both Knox and Dad on his balcony. I loved getting to help the two forge a relationship together. To show Knox what love looks like . . . and maybe what I hope he'll do for me when I get older.

* * *

I began to call him Rod. The transition from calling him Dad to Rod was subtle and unnoticed until Adam mentioned it in passing. "Why have you started calling him Rod lately?" he asked one night during dinner.

I think it was a way for my brain to subconsciously set boundaries and, in doing so, protect me. He didn't feel like Dad anymore. When the man who used to change my diapers, sing me to sleep, and stop monsters from coming into my room now depended on me for some of those things, the dynamics changed. I matured, and he grew older. Those were two different things. Perhaps this would have happened even if the stoke hadn't. But this was my nuanced normal now.

His love for his family never wavered; his sense of humour remained the same as it was before the stroke. The sound of his voice was the same, and despite a further receding hairline, he still looked like Dad.

But the man that I'd grown to take care of, to respect in a new way, was no longer a dad I recognized. I was grieving the loss of a parent who was still here, pre-emptively saying goodbye. I was now protecting the man I once knew to be my protector. Providing for one who once was my provider. In some ways, the things were taken away that made him Dad. He held the title of father, but no longer of Dad in my head.

Rod needed help with his finances; Dad paid his mortgage. Rod couldn't remember where he'd parked his car; Dad could change an alternator. The difference in behaviour and ability was as stark as the name change.

After much, much counselling, I began to realize that calling him Rod was an attempt to dissociate, to prevent more pain. Every appointment with Rod, every call from him, felt like my Band-Aid was being ripped off. The reality of what I thought a father was supposed to be was no longer. Instead, I was loving and caring for a person who couldn't fulfill the fatherly role in the way he once had.

Selfish. Resentful. Angry. Disrespectful. Unloving. When applied to me, all those labels are true. I thought I deserved a dad for life and that I needed a dad now. Instead, I got a Rod. What I failed to see was the obvious: he was both. And, if he had his way, he would always be Dad. This wasn't what he wanted, nor did he ask for it. All he wanted was to love me in the way I needed to be. I chose to take that title away from him when he had earned it and was actually living up to it in his own way.

And in being so wrapped up in my own pain, I was forgetting to enjoy the moments that Dad was still here. I was too busy grieving what I thought I'd lost. And the person I thought I'd lost.

The dad who would pick up the phone anytime I called, even when he was in a client meeting, was still there. He always answered. His brain used to spin marvellously imaginative bedtime stories. That same imagination produced what I now called "lies." Maybe I just grew jaded enough to stop seeing the magic. As a teen, the dad who would listen to every problem I had and give his advice was still true today. He listens, and I continue to ignore parts of his advice. Partly because I'm not sure I trust the source, and partly because I'm internally still a willful teenager. Dad would attend everything, always my biggest supporter. And he still does that for my kids. I just have to drive him.

In writing this, I am beginning to see that Rod is still Dad. His traits that I needed as a child are still true today. They just manifest differently. And that's not his fault. It's on me that I can't always see him for who he is. That he's Dad. The qualities that made him remain, even if sometimes hidden or hard to see.

* * *

In some ways, caring for parents gives you a little glimpse into the future of raising your kids. Beyond the commonalities of diaper changes (which, thank goodness, have not been since Dad was in the hospital), there are other similarities. Like you can easily replicate the challenges or conversations that you have with your father by having them with your son.

When Dad was in cardiac rehab at Laurel Place back in 2015, he had regular homework to do. Each day, his schedule consisted of sessions with his occupational therapist, short workouts with his physiotherapist, and the occasional coffee run with Daryl. It was predictable. To maintain his progress, the therapists often assigned him homework to do on his own. Often this was a deductive reasoning sheet where he received two statements and needed to draw a conclusion. And the other common worksheet was mental math. Think about the ones you did in elementary school where you had to answer as many addition, subtraction, or easy multiplication questions as you could in one minute. Those sheets were exactly what my middle-aged father was now completing. Exercises designed to challenge his thinking and support his daily living. Effectively, it was re-teaching his brain the skills that generally come fairly naturally to most adults.

It was a sunny afternoon as I punched in the code to let myself into the locked-down facility. Walking down the hallway, Dad's sweatshirt was visible at his seat in the dining room, head down like he was concentrating. Sneakily, I slowly walked toward him, peering around his shoulder to see the math he was working on. Imagine my surprise when I see him doing the mental math problems with a calculator on his iPod! The problems that were supposed to be challenging his brain were being solved by a free app.

Now, part of me was actually proud. He was smart enough to remember how to cheat, and likely get away with it. The other part of me, disappointed. Could he not solve 7+6 by himself? Were things that far gone?

I felt as though I had to have a conversation with him about it, and in true Quiring fashion, use sarcasm as the basis for it all. That particular skill never has and likely will never leave him.

"Hey, crazy old man," I started, using my newest term of endearment for him. I would like to be clear that he did, in fact, like that name.

"Hey, crazy young girl," he replied.

"Dad, are you really using a calculator to do your homework? Your occupational therapist is going to kill you. You know this work is supposed to help your brain get better, but you're cheating."

"I am not cheating! I outsmarted the homework, and she will never know," he almost shouted at me.

"And you know what God says about cheaters, right Dad?" I retorted.

He chuckled and then continued on with his homework, calculator app still turned on.

This conversation, I can only assume, foreshadows ones to come with my own children.

The challenges of caring for Dad have and will continue to prepare me for my role as a parent. In setting boundaries with Dad, I've learned what acceptable risk looks like for my children. That failure is sometimes a success. Dad's questions about God and heaven are mirrored in his grandson's four-year-old mind. My patience, granted throughout Dad's recovery, has stretched and extended as my kids become more vocal. While I can't very well discipline Dad and send him to a time-out when he says something inappropriate or hurtful, I am learning how to talk through it. How to navigate conflict when we simply swept it under the rug as we grew up. Because of his example as a father, and my experience with him as a dependent, my confidence as a parent has grown.

* * *

I've learned that some families are open about some things, and others about different things. For example, my family had no problem discussing finances. Conflict and feelings, however, was a completely different story. Those we swept under the rug and ignored. Perhaps it was our discomfort with it, perhaps it was a generational thing. Regardless, it was what happened. Other families in my life are completely comfortable with conflict. They embrace it as a chance to grow. But ask them what their net income is and they'll look at you like you have two heads. Believe me, it's happened.

True caregiving requires uncomfortable questions.

"Have you pooped today?"

"Are you sexually active?"

"Is there anything coming out of holes in your body that shouldn't be coming out of holes in your body?"

All the questions you don't want your doctor to ask you that you are now asking your parent. It's awkward.

And beyond just the questions themselves, it's the regularity with which you have to ask. These aren't one and done type questions. Weekly or monthly, they form as normal a part of your conversation as asking how the weather is. They become routine in cadence, though the uncomfortableness never leaves. And if the person responding has any sort of dementia or memory impairment, the integrity of their responses is always in question. So you ask more. You invade more. Their privacy becomes less and less for the necessity of medicine.

In taking care of Dad, my boundaries around information and asking questions were extremely far away. Yes, the questions made me extremely awkward. Awkward and I do not get along. I watch *The Office* and I hide under a blanket because Michael Scott makes me so uncomfortable. But somehow, I'm fine to ask Dad all these questions.

Until . . . I'm not.

When I hit that boundary—which, for me, is anything related to the working of his male parts—Cody steps in. I have no idea what's said or how it's asked. I simply get a text from my brother that says, "Everything is good with Dad." I fully exhale and move on. Yet another of the million reasons I am grateful to have a brother, to have Cody on my team.

I'm sure these questions frustrate Dad. I don't want to ask them. And I'm equally confident that he doesn't want to answer them. Some days I feel like his nursemaid. Or worse, his prosecutor. Badgering him with questions that cause stammers and inconsistencies in responses. At the attempt to get to the truth, I dig. I interrogate.

My wonderfully insightful counsellor, Tracey, recommended that I use a skill she called compassionate curiosity. In my googling of it after our session, I learned that it is a capability from trauma-informed teaching. It means asking things out of a genuine place of empathy and curiosity, remembering that I don't know all the answers or the "why" behind Dad's actions. Compassion and interrogation are often at odds. For us, this looked practically like this:

Instead of asking, "Any issues with your bladder today?" we tried, "How are things going today, Dad?"

We substituted "Do you want to go to counselling?" with "What is helping you cope, Dad?"

We rephrased "Dad, you need to stop driving," into "Dad, why is it so important to you to have access to a vehicle?"

Sometimes, I find, it's the dread of what's coming next or what you have to address that's the worst. Dad often handles things better than I give him credit for, or is stronger than I thought he would be. And I'm sure he gripes about me to his ladies he lunches with. Remember how excited we all were to get our licenses? It's so much worse losing them.

I can guarantee that these questions are not completely true to the approach of compassionate curiosity that Tracey proposed. There's a whole realm of science behind it that I'm not well-versed in. But take my advice from a practical rather than scientific point of view. It's less about what you ask than how you ask it. Ask, don't tell. Assume the best rather than the worst. Actually, assume you know nothing.

And don't have an agenda. When I turned the questions into ones to genuinely understand Dad more, we not only deepened our relationship, but the other pieces came out anyway.

And isn't that the most loving thing to do?

* * *

It would be remiss of me to not acknowledge our family's privilege. We are upper-middle class, white, university-educated individuals. We are incredibly blessed and privileged by winning the lottery of birth to have been born in Canada, into the circumstances we were. Yes, my family worked hard. No, we didn't come from significant generational wealth. But we are incredibly privileged.

That privilege results in significant supports when it comes to taking care of Dad. Some are available to anyone in the province of British Columbia. Others are covered by my parents' extended health insurance. Yet we paid for more supports out of pocket because we were able to.

There's our work. Adam and I, in particular, were privileged to work for companies with supportive managers who gave us all the paid or unpaid time off they could. Especially since the pandemic, we are able to work from home and attend appointments as needed. No one has ever questioned our whereabouts or whom appointments are for. Yes, we still have to catch up on work in evenings, and yes, we take a lot of meetings in the car. But this too is privilege.

This is not the case for so many, and we recognize how fortunate this makes us. Cody was granted much time off from work, and even flights from Mom's employer to come and visit in the tough weeks. Carlee, as a teacher, has it tougher. Her personal days are few and far between, making it incredibly challenging for her to come to BC outside of school holidays. But even during school holidays, flight prices have never been a deal breaker for our family coming to support. For that and so much more, we are extremely privileged.

When Dad immediately came out of rehab, the social worker set us up with someone called a community support worker. Due to the nature of Dad's traumatic brain injury, he qualified for support a few days a week. This rotating person would come for several hours, twice a week, to take Dad on walks, out for coffee, and get him reintegrated into society. Usually it was a female-identifying person. She would help Dad make dinner or go through his homework.

His homework came from an outpatient occupational therapy program. At first, Dad's extended health insurance covered this through a community clinic. Dad would drive himself twice a month to the clinic and work through memory exercises and situational analyses. He saw minimal improvement and, unfortunately, the therapist would not release his case notes or information to me.

You see, Dad had to consent to sharing information with me, as part of allowing him his own boundaries, and he would provide his consent some days but on others, he refused. It was infuriating. How could I know how to support him and challenge him at home if I didn't have the information? It didn't seem to matter.

The first occupational therapy clinic was good, but then we got a second, private occupational therapist who was wonderful. Bailey is a friend of a friend. She is smart and sarcastic, two qualities that endeared her to my dad right away. Her focus became improving Dad's brain function. It wasn't counselling, though in my mind that was something he desperately needed. It was all about helping him remember. So that he could forget.

He needed to forget that he couldn't do things in order to do them. He always struggled to maintain confidence, and the more he thought he was failing, the lower his confidence became. This likely increased his already high anxiety and depression. Plus, the added frustration impacted his traumatic brain injury and made his memory worse. It was a cycle of catastrophe in a sense. There were no winners.

Bailey worked with Dad for years. She had initially cautioned that his brain injury appeared severe and seeing any improvement was unlikely. Bailey was cautious in managing our expectations and, as a result, exceeded them. She coached Dad to solve problems. He was floundering, and she caught him. We saw improvement that most would quantify as little. We saw them as massive.

Like the time Dad's car battery wouldn't hold a charge. He was so frustrated and constantly needed Adam to come over and jump him so he could go to the McDonald's drive-thru. Using the lessons he learned from Bailey, he took initiative. He researched a portable booster pack and where he could buy it. Then he asked me to take him. Every single one of these steps was incredibly difficult for his brain, but he did it. Little wins in most books, huge in his.

The community support worker was funded for a few months before the government deemed that Dad was able to live and function independently. To me, that seemed like a stretch. Their definition of "fine" was wildly different from mine. "Able to live" to the government meant able to bathe and eat on his own. The same term, to me, meant a return to normal, or what had been. Though in hindsight, living independently was different from living as he had previously. Dad was more than capable of washing himself. He could get food into his system—the government didn't care if it was takeout pizza or a homemade dinner. Dad could walk without assistance, albeit slowly. By their criteria, he was "fine."

By mine, he was anything but.

So we continued to scaffold him. We secured a regular cleaner to make sure that his house was clean and would keep him healthy. For a while, meals arrived from every delivery service we could find, even though Dad preferred to pick up take-out. He would drive to his old engineering firm, where his amazing team set up a workstation in the conference room for him to reacquaint himself with the technology they used. The routine of work calmed him and gave him purpose.

Even if the drawings he was engineering never went past the printer he'd forget to pick them up from.

He had a trainer, one who knew him before his stroke. She worked on a low impact program for him to improve his heart health, though he viewed their training sessions as a strengthening of his voice rather than his biceps. He talked more than he lifted. All of these things were an investment in his health. In his recovery.

For a short period of time, Dad attended a stroke survivor support group. A small group of five or six survivors sat in a room, drank coffee, and reminisced about how they were coping. The wins, the losses. They laughed a bit. Dad came home after his fourth session, reflecting openly.

"Rayel, I'm so lucky. Those people are way worse off than I am. I can still talk, still walk. There are so many friends around us who help me. There's money in my account. I'm a lucky one compared to them."

Despite everything that happened, he saw what I couldn't. Dad saw his blessings. I was so focused on what we'd lost, on what we had to do to get Dad "back to normal," that I couldn't see what was right in front of me. We had him. He had us.

No matter how much we invested to make Dad's life easier, better, or safer, it wouldn't change that simple fact. He was here. He was loved.

* * *

In the era of smartphones, email, and being bombarded with technology, scams run rampant. It seems the Canada Revenue Agency calls me every day, threatening me with jail time because I haven't paid my taxes. But if I pay them $5,000 over the phone, I'll be in the clear. Or I'll get texts from a bank I don't use, asking me to click a link to verify a bank transfer. Being clear-headed (most of the time) and rational (occasionally), I know enough not to fall for any of these scams.

And you can imagine how much harder that is for someone with a diminished mental capacity. Someone with a traumatic brain injury. Someone with dementia, anxiety, or a host of other things that make this enticing.

This was just as true for Dad.

Adam, our resident accountant, would often get phone calls from Dad.

"Adam! Have you paid my taxes? The CRA told me that I'm going to jail. I trusted you!"

"Rod," Adam would reply, "you are good. It's paid. This is a scam. If they need something, they'll write to us."

Dad would breathe his sigh of relief and move on.

Until the next week, when the same call would come from the alleged tax authorities, and Dad would make identical calls to his son-in-law.

It took a few months before Dad realized that this wasn't the way tax collectors worked.

Caregiving can be terrifying, especially when you see the people you love being taken advantage of. I've seen someone on the periphery of my dad's life watch as he does his online banking, noting his account balances. Perhaps even his passwords. I can't be certain. A stranger that put herself in a position to befriend him and, absolute worst case scenario, rob him. It was, I hope, an innocent situation. The two were having coffee at Starbucks and Dad, suddenly worried about whether he'd paid a bill, logged into his app to check.

On this occasion when we noticed someone could possibly take advantage of Dad's diminished capacity and moderate accounts, we put safeguards in place. We contacted lawyers to ensure no one could transfer properties without my notification. Our wealth managers implemented a two-step authentication, which included me, so no one could access

Dad's investments. We reduced his credit limit, trying to protect his assets, without him realizing anything had happened. We didn't want to create alarm, for him or others, where there didn't need to be.

So we had to focus on educating. Reminding Dad of online safety, of personal safety. We found a line where he could be free but where we could stop the worst from happening. It was a way of ensuring his independence, with some guardrails. Acceptable risk. What could we withstand happening, maybe as a learning experience for Dad, without compromising his foundational safety?

How could we keep his foundation secure and be his safety net and let him continue to take risks and grow?

Harkening back to my Psych 101 days, Maslow has this hierarchy of needs that pretty much says that you are motivated by certain psychological needs, the most basic of which is physiological (think food, water, or shelter) and safety. I'd like to point out that I scored a 64% in Psych 101, with grading on a curve, so take this for what it's worth. But my premise is this: the basics of his safety, the sense of security that Dad needed, were important. If we could ensure his safety was secure, maybe he'd be motivated to attain higher things—like friendships or gaining self-esteem. Maybe, if we kept his foundation stable, he could get his confidence back. Dare I say his mojo?

In another instance, someone hacked Dad's social media. We still aren't sure how or why, and we rationalize it happening with the platitude that it can happen to anyone. It showed up as it usually does, with weird messages being sent via the platform. Cody noticed it first and quickly called so we could form a plan. Cody navigated yet another online security talk with Dad, while I got a VPN, credit monitoring, and enhanced identify theft protection placed on his online accounts.

These matters seem trivial, but add them all up, and it was a lot.

* * *

018: A BOX OF CHOCOLATES

These emotions and the constant toll on our schedule led to the inevitable burnout. There was simply not enough time or counselling to deal with everything that was being thrown at us. I avoided friends. My text message inbox was in the triple digits with unread messages. Sleep, oh, that precious sleep, was elusive again.

My compassion well was dry. I couldn't force myself to feel empathy, or even to want to. I catastrophized every situation. Each phone call turned into thoughts that it was Dad's last to me. I pulled back from the things that made me happy, from the people who made me happy. Adam and I became roommates instead of spouses. We talked, but intimacy and affection were a nonstarter. Wine pours became heavier. Anger appeared when patience ran out, which was quickly. I felt like I was operating at 30% of who I was, or who I wanted to be. And the best of that 30% went to my kids. Which, by my limited math skills, meant the remaining 10% went to my husband, my work, and my community.

I wasn't exercising. I certainly wasn't praying.

The burnout was real. I didn't recognize it because I was too busy. I covered up the sleeplessness with Zopiclone. My friends graciously accepted all the excuses I could make up for why I didn't want to attend girls' night. Dinners just couldn't get made. It wasn't that I didn't have the time, just no desire. Coffee couldn't fuel me. The exhaustion was real. There was no worship song, no amount of baths and certainly no amount of wine that would make me feel anything but numb.

But it wasn't busy-ness that I was experiencing; it was anxiety. It was depression. I wish I had been busy taking care of myself, but I wasn't. My calendar was full of appointments for others. My thumbs glued to my phone screen, scrolling mindlessly. As much as I ignored my own needs, I also ignored Adam.

For years, Adam had been quietly supporting in every conceivable way. He'd borne the brunt of my emotional outbursts, the direct recipient of my anger simply because he was physically the closest to me. Adam had taken on every job I'd asked of him without being thanked, without being recognized. He'd done his job well. Our family was surviving because of him. Unfortunately, he'd become lower on my priority list than either of us might have liked.

And still, he never complained. The kids and Dad took up most of my time, with the remainder being spent on work and commitments with friends or volunteer endeavours. Date nights were once a week, after the kids were in bed, with sushi on the couch. We'd turn a show on and intentionally not talk because I was exhausted and he was respectful of that. When we did talk, it was often me venting. Sometimes about his family, sometimes about mine. Often, about him.

I have no magical answer for how I put Adam first and heavily invested in our marriage. I don't. We continue to work together to tackle the responsibilities of being some of the first people we know in the sandwich generation. We focus on working together as a team, trusting that the love and intimacy are still there when we need it. When we can get back to it.

Sometimes you just need to know that you have someone in your corner. Someone willing to be the sandwich with you instead of taking another bite out of you.

* * *

Being in the middle of raising your kids and caring for your parents is sometimes impossible. It's a terrible kind of sandwich. It's like Cheez Whiz and jam—which, by the way, Dad would occasionally slip into my school lunches. Nasty, sticky. It can make a mess, just like in our relationships, if we're not careful.

Being in the middle pulls on your relationships. You evaluate and shift priorities daily, if not hourly. Unexpected calls, unanswered texts. Burnout, depression. It's all the reality of being the sandwich generation.

Resiliency is key to surviving in this in-between place. It's not a constant state of resiliency but a learned skill. Self-care is a word that is thrown around on Instagram that I vehemently disagreed with. *Ain't no one got time for that!* I'd regularly think. The age-old travel concept of "putting on your own mask before assisting others" didn't resonate. In spending all my energy looking after others, I neglected myself. It resulted in medication to make me sleep and antidepressants that brought me back.

I grew up with parents who did not believe in mental illness. Maybe it was less that they didn't believe in it, more that they didn't know about it. Ignorant even. "Depression" was not a word in their vocabulary. Counselling was not common, nor do I think it was ever truly considered by them as individuals or a couple. It was a combination of their own upbringing, their generation. They valued being able to achieve, to get through whatever came.

When Dad was first in rehab, he was prescribed mood medication for his anxiety and depression. Mom's top priority was to get him weaned from the meds, saying they were unnecessary and would change him as a person. Once she died, I took that baton and reiterated the same goal to Dad's psychiatrist. We tried to wean Dad, and it did not go well. His worries came back with a vengeance, as did his subsequent number of phone calls to me. It was clear that his medication was key to functioning and healing. So back on them he went.

There is absolutely nothing wrong with getting help. I know that now. It took some crashes and burns in my own life to figure that one out. My medications changed my outlook and likely prevented me from hurting myself further. Counselling became a welcome part of my month instead of a dreaded one. Exercise, prayer, cooking after the kids went to bed—these were all just little ways that I could do something for myself. Regular showers became a game changer. Occasionally, I even remembered to drink water instead of coffee and wine. My stylist went to work on my hair more than once a year. And my mental health needed it all.

* * *

Being stuck in the sandwich generation is emotionally exhausting. You experience the best and worst of life with those you love. Your patience runs thin from your toddler's emotional outbursts, only to be challenged again by repetitive conversations with a parent. The candle literally burns at both ends. It might feel like you deserve a break, but one never comes. Or you simply never take it. The weight of worry is heavy. The appointments and commitments are overwhelming. Thousands of responsibilities rest on your shoulders.

No one gets the best of you.

You push, you strive, you try to put one foot in front of the other. The days feel endless. The hope, fickle at best. There is guilt and shame. Questions of wondering whether you are doing enough, being enough, wander through your head.

And some days, it's just apathy. You stick your head in the sand, refusing to feel at all. You distract yourself with anything and everything that will allow you to turn your brain off. Feeling nothing feels better than feeling something.

This is my experience, and maybe it's yours too. Maybe it's your friends' or your partner's. You might be in the thick of it, or you might be waiting on the edge for the proverbial shoe to drop. There's no one way to feel. You'll feel it all at different points. The commonality between our experiences is this: love is in the middle of this beautifully painful sandwich.

We love our kids and our parents. Some days we love them more than others. Occasionally, we love them but don't like them all that much. But we wouldn't be where we are without love. We made a choice, despite all circumstances. Love is painful, but it is also beautiful.

Being the sandwich generation is such a hard good. Despite all you've just read, I wouldn't trade it. I have Dad. He's here. He gives me hugs. He loves me. My kids have core memories with him. We have family photos that will live on long after he goes. I still call him when I can't remember how to unclog a toilet (YouTube be damned!). He doesn't want to be living with a traumatic brain injury. I get to show my kids how I hope they'll take care of me someday.

But mostly, I get my dad. To connect with him, learn from him. I watch his hands move so I can remember the quiver of his thumb when it no longer moves. I put my head on his shoulder, smelling his Ivory soap and burning that sensory memory into my brain. His steps slow, and I remember how sure they used to be. His eyes droop, but the sparkle of a good joke remains. He is still here. He is still with me. And that's enough to keep me going.

So why do I do what I do? Partly it's out of obligation, but overwhelmingly, it's out of affection. My crazy old man was my first love. There is nothing that I wouldn't do for him because that's exactly what he would do for me. I love that he appreciates it. I'm grateful he recognizes all our efforts. It's a way for me to thank him and pay him back in a way for everything he did to help me become who I am today. It's a privilege, a sometimes awful one, but a privilege nonetheless. Our relationship is markedly different than at any other stage of my life. Maybe it would have been that way even if he hadn't had his stroke and heart attack, but this is what I know now. This is who he is now, and as much as I try to imagine our life if this hadn't happened, I can't know for certain what it would be like.

It is my greatest joy to love my dad and my kids. It's the hardest job I've ever done. There's no performance review. I have no idea if I'm doing it right, or even remotely succeeding. But they smile. They are here. They tell me they love me. I love them. That's all that I need.

019: HEARTS THAT FAIL

Six and a half years had passed since Mom died. There were so many firsts, so many lasts. New babies, new homes, new memories that she was no longer a part of. Adam and I had been on trips around the world, and we'd been to winery after winery, but in both cases, she wasn't there to reminisce with. We'd made big decisions without her guidance and mentorship, succeeding and failing on our own.

Throughout this time, Dad had regular checkups for his heart. He'd had twice-yearly cardiologist appointments to review his medications and also his symptoms. At one appointment in late 2016, due to a lack of improvement in Dad's heart function, the doctor recommended that Dad have a cardioverter-defibrillator surgically implanted. This device was slightly different from a pacemaker in that it would shock Dad's heart back into rhythm if it stopped again, effectively mitigating the aftereffects of a heart attack.

So a few months later, we made the now-familiar trek down Highway 1 to Royal Columbian Hospital for a day procedure to have his ICD implanted. Dad was nervous, tapping his thumbs together the entire drive, the same habit he'd developed since his stroke. He kept repeating the same stories and questions; when Dad's memory is even more impaired than normal, we know anxiety is at its peak. As we registered and got settled in his room, he held my hand. His was cold but strong, gripping tightly as though he was a lost little boy who didn't know what to do. We chatted while the nurses prepped him, and all the while, he held my hand. As they wheeled him out to the operating room, Dad smiled a half smile at me and told me, "I'll be okay, Rayel. I'll see you soon." Even in the hardest of moments for him, he was still Dad, and he was still trying to take care of me.

The procedure lasted only half an hour or so, and he was back up in his room, hair net on (which was ironic because the hair on his head was virtually non-existent). They'd given him a mild sedative, so his hands were still, and his half-smile was lazy but apparent. "I'm so proud of you," I whispered to him. "You did it!" In response, he took my hand again and closed his eyes for a little nap.

Despite having the ICD as an "in case of emergency" backup plan, we still needed to have Dad in for heart monitoring every so often. Each year, he would go for an echocardiogram, nuclear stress test, or some other form of monitoring to see how his heart pumping function was progressing and to make sure there were no other blockages. In October 2020, an echocardiogram revealed that Dad's left ventricle was only pumping at 30% efficiency. Normal heart pumping function should be at least 60%. This reduced pumping efficiency is called heart failure. While there are a variety of medications that can help the heart recover and slow its progress, this is a serious diagnosis. The prognosis is marked with increasing symptom burden, decreased quality of life, and frequent hospitalizations in its late stages.

At Dad's regular checkup one year later, we mentioned that he was beginning to feel winded easily, sweat profusely, and have difficulty sleeping unless he was sitting up. These symptoms were worrisome to the doctor and I, but not to Dad. Blissful ignorance is truly a gift. Because of these reports, Dad returned to the familiar cardiac catheterization lab at Royal Columbian for an angiogram to rule out any additional blockages as well as understand where his heart pumping function was at.

Our friend, Perry, took Dad on the day of the appointment. As COVID-19 was still running wild, and I had a runny nose, our household was stuck at home. Dad was understandably nervous and regularly needed to be reminded of what was happening. He told the nurses that he didn't know why he was there, only that his daughter forced him to be. Perry quietly slipped out after his intake to let the nurses know the entire situation, while also trying to keep Dad's dignity intact. The procedure was more invasive than we let on to Dad, and after that, there was a swift response from him.

"Rayel, I am never letting that happen again. I felt violated and I will not have any more tests done."

At first I shook my head, chalking this up to an old man's eccentricities. However, as his complaints became more regular and even louder, I realized that perhaps there was something more to this. Perhaps Dad didn't care anymore. And as it turns out, there was a reason for that. Maybe, without being told, he knew the prognosis after all.

Several weeks after the procedure, the cardiologist brought us back to his office to review the results.

"Well, there is no block that needs a stent, so that's good," he began, speaking to Dad. "But it looks like one of your stents became occluded, and your body built a collateral artery to get by."

"Excuse me?" I interrupted.

"Your dad's heart created its own bypass. It is flowing blood around the block so the heart can still move blood. It's quite phenomenal," he remarked.

"But how is his heart pumping function then?" I asked.

"Ahh. Let me look." He peered at his computer screen, scrolling through the post-procedure report. "It looks like the heart pumping function is at about 20% of normal. That's not good. And it's down from his last echocardiogram."

"I don't understand," I said firmly. "What does this mean for his heart?"

"Your father is in heart failure," the doctor said with a small smile on his face.

It was a diagnosis I knew was coming but one I couldn't bear to hear said out loud. There was no other explanation, and I knew that, but it didn't make it easier. As I looked at the doctor, the smile was still on his face. It was like he was trying to stay positive, that a smile could fix the wound that his words had just inflicted.

"So what's the prognosis? What can I expect next?" I almost yelled.

"It's hard to say because there are many variables and much can change with medication these days, but typically, 50% of patients with this stage of heart failure won't make it beyond five years."

There is a benefit to having a traumatic brain injury like Dad's, and that is that you don't often dwell on difficult news for long. As we drove home, each lost in our own thoughts, I asked Dad if he knew what had just happened.

"I have no idea. I can't remember anything he said," Dad remarked.

"Well, Dad, you are in heart failure," I said softly.

"I am?!" he breathed desperately. "So I'm dying?"

How do you answer that? How do you tell your own father that he is dying and dying sooner than we ever dreamed? Slowly, very slowly.

"Dad, I don't know how to tell you this." I tried to soften the blow and did so awkwardly. "We are all dying. But you are dying faster, I guess. Yes, you are dying, Dad. I'm so sorry."

He stared out the window, seemingly deep in thought. Thirty seconds later, he responded in the way I expected from a man with an ongoing memory impairment.

"Where are your kids today?"

The singular benefit to a brain like Dad's: he doesn't focus on bad news for long.

I texted Katie a few weeks later and asked for her professional advice on Dad's condition and what I could expect to fail next in this journey of heart failure. She suggested that we meet with all of our kids at a park and we could talk while they played.

One stunning Saturday morning, Adam and I drove with the kids to Vancouver and met Katie, who brought her boys, coffee, and treats. Katie is one of the most compassionate people I know, listening so deeply to things not said and fears not spoken. She is an excellent doctor equally because of her brains as her heart, and on this day, I needed both.

As we pushed our toddlers on the swings, I gave her the updates on Dad, his health, his test results, and the doctor's prognosis. After a bit of back and forth, I asked the most pointed question I could: "Katie, how long do we have?"

She paused for a moment and took a breath. "Ray, I like to give my patients their prognosis in terms of years, months, weeks, or days. From everything you've said, and remember that I haven't seen the reports myself, I'd say your dad is in the months to year category." She stopped pushing and looked through my eyes and into my heart. "I am so sorry," she said.

It's one thing when a doctor tells you bad news. It's entirely another when your best friend, who is a brilliant doctor, who knows all of your fears, and who has been alongside you the entire journey, tells you bad news. When Katie said this, she knew it wasn't just about planning for the rest of Dad's life. She knew it was about grieving what he will miss. She knew it was about preparing his grandchildren for a life without him. The news would inevitably bring pain and memories linked to Mom. And deep down, I think she realized that this would rip my heart out, causing more questions than answers. But she did it anyway, because that's what friends do. They give you the truth, and then they help you pick up the pieces.

* * *

There were people who told me that I needed to have faith because we have a God who can heal and who is not beholden to a doctor's knowledge and prognosis. There were others who boldly stated that God would provide a miracle and Dad would experience healing: he had come this far. Why would God take him now? It equal parts made me feel guilty and hopeful. I prayed for faith. Wasn't I given enough of it?

I do believe that our God is one who heals and one who is holy over all. That He grants miracles. His goodness undeniable. I know that Jesus experienced grief and wept bitterly over the loss of those close to him.

And even so, what I also know is that I have been through the death of a parent before.

I intimately know the pain associated with watching the person who is supposed to care for you slip away beyond help. I know the number of tears that come with watching your expectations and hopes for your parent's future be stripped away by ventilators and IV poles. The gut-wrenching, breath-taking, bone-crushing pain that comes with releasing your parent from everything here on earth and giving them the freedom to depart for heaven is one I'm intimately familiar with. There's the hurt that comes with feeling abandoned, of being left behind without any understanding as to why. Anger. Bitterness that abounds in grief. I know the blame game, the resentment, and the questioning that slaps you in the face just when you think you are through the worst of your grief. Tension that caring for someone you love puts on your other relationships, testing them and threatening them in every way.

So I sit on this middle ground, asking myself if I have enough faith. I ask myself if I am doubting God or if I am smartly preparing for the inevitable. Am I hoping enough? Praying enough? Maybe my lack of faith is the reason for all this, for the heartache and pain we've gone through the last seven years. I question God's purpose in this, but not His goodness, because my faith is bigger than my feelings.

And what I know, beyond a shadow of a doubt, is that I love my dad. I love him deeply and fully, unconditionally. So no matter how hard it hurts, no matter what the prognosis or how many days of him I have left, I am walking forward with him. I am walking to the park to watch him push his grandchildren on the swing. We will shuffle together down the escalator as we take an airplane to visit Cody, Carlee, and their children. Together, trudging through the unknowns and the yet-to-bes. Because I have a God who never leaves me and who loves me. So I will never leave you, Dad, and I love you forever.

Walking headfirst into hardship is a choice, and a terrifying one. Who wants more heartache and work? But after everything we've been through, I know these things to be true: you are never alone and love is always worth it.

EPILOGUE

Knox slowly began asking questions about heaven and Jesus as he was going to bed. At first, Adam and I thought that it was a stall tactic, anything to keep us from leaving the room and the monsters from coming out from under his bed. But the questions became more regular, more persistent in their demands for a response. Each night, some variation of these were asked, and sometimes all of them asked in rapid-fire succession.

"Where does Grandma live?"

"Why did Jesus die?"

"How many toys are in heaven?"

"Does Jesus piggyback us to heaven when we die?"

The typical questions of a three-year-old who is trying to grasp a theological concept that many adults question and struggle with on a daily basis. But one day, the conversation shifted ever so slightly. Knox was supposed to be asleep half an hour earlier, but he was so excited that our friend was over for dinner that it took him a while to wind down. As I went upstairs for the third time, ready to deliver a consequence for not staying in his bed, he grabbed my neck and asked me a question.

"Mom," he asked in his high-pitched, little boy voice. "I don't want to be alone."

"Oh, baby, you'll never be alone. Mom and Dad are always here, and so is Jesus. He never leaves you."

He thought for a moment and then responded, "What about when I die?"

"Well, if you die and Jesus is your friend who lives in your heart, you get to go to heaven."

"Where Grandma lives?" he asked curiously.

"Yeah, buddy, where Grandma lives." I smiled in the dark, thinking of Mom looking down on this conversation with a glass of wine in hand, being overjoyed that Knox was wondering about Jesus.

"Okay, then I want to go to heaven someday. I don't want to be alone."

His decisiveness caught me by surprise. "Well, buddy, that means you have to ask Jesus to come and live in your heart."

"Okay." He closed his eyes and quickly said, "Jesus, please come into my heart."

"Wait a sec. Knox, do you think Jesus is God's son?" I asked cautiously.

"Yeah."

I probed further. "And do you think Jesus died for all the bad things you've done?"

"I haven't done any bad things, Mom!" His self-awareness was clearly still developing.

I smiled and let out a chuckle. "Okay, what about for all the bad things that you'll probably do?"

"Yeah, he died for that."

"And do you think Jesus is in heaven now?" I looked deep into his eyes.

He nodded. "Yeah, my Bible says that when we read that story."

I couldn't think of anything else to ask to assess if he was ready to take what I knew was a huge step in his faith journey. "Well, then I guess you just have to pray and ask Jesus to live in your heart."

Very matter-of-factually, he responded, "Yeah, I don't want to be alone." He closed his eyes again. "Jesus, thanks for dying for the bad things. Will you please come live in my heart so I can go to heaven?"

As I walked downstairs to tell Adam what I had just been witness to, my shock was visible. My eyes were wide, my mouth was open, and I couldn't focus on anything until I had got these words out: "Our son became a Christian tonight."

I believe the party in heaven that night was loud was full of excitement and led as equally by Jesus as it was by Mom. Her grandson's eternity is secure. His hope is in Jesus.

Knox and Savvy will never know their grandma on earth. They will never know her warmth, her wit, or her commitment to success. Her Oreo cookies will be made by a recipe rather than by her hands. Her excessively loud snores won't make them laugh because they won't hear them. She will be absent in pictures of their kindergarten graduations and weddings. They would have loved her just as she would have loved them.

But "Grandma in heaven," as we've started calling her, lives on. Her quotes, legacy, and memory live on in her friends, in her siblings, and in her nieces and nephews.

They live on in Cody. His ability to work hard and rest hard comes from her. His sarcasm and impatience on the road also are hers. He has the red facial hair from the Isaak side, and Mom's sense of adventure. Her heart for others lives on in him, and her quiet faith is mirrored in his own. Cody is Emily's son and Emily's legacy, through and through.

Mom's memory lives on in Dad. In the ring that lives on his finger, symbolizing their commitment to one another. We regularly talk about "What would Emily do?" when we make decisions or tease one another. Her legacy lives on in the way that Dad loves and supports those he loves, fully and deeply.

Mom's memory lives on in her siblings, nieces, and nephews. In the stories they tell and the way they take care of our nuclear family. Her commitment to family, weathering all the storms, pandemics, and life that comes in between relationships, remains steadfast in her extended family. In the people who share her blood.

Mom's legacy lives on in her friends. In those who take her patterns and yarn and create new blankets for her grandchildren. She is alongside those who wear her clothes and shoes. Her legacy is strengthened with each toast of limoncello or bottle of deep and delicious red wine. Through those who play beautiful music on her piano and teach little ones to do the same. Her heart beats with those who care for her children and grandchildren as though they were their own. She did not leave us alone.

Mom's legacy lives on in her grandkids. As they learn to follow Jesus and walk in faith, they are inheriting direct lessons from Mom's life. Her death and eternal life in heaven open the door to conversations with the next generation about faith, death, and salvation. As desperately as I wish she was here to tell them herself, the very fact she is absent makes the lesson that much more powerful.

And Mom will live on in me. In the best of me and worst of me, she will live. Her hospitality and generosity of time and money are genetic, and ones I am proud to bear. Her courage and independence, both the good aspects and challenging ones, flourish in me. Like her, I love my family. I aspire to success. We share goals and dreams, professionally and personally. Plus, I'll never stop looking like her.

* * *

There's no manual for how to respond to a dying parent. This is the prime example of a sandwicher. You can't save them. You can't change things. I couldn't outwork this, outthink this. It was an impossible problem to solve. It's about love, compassion, and truth at this point. Responding that you can't do anything but you love them, you're with them. Holding their hand like they held yours. Kissing their cheeks and just being with them during this nightmare. The same way they calmed you during yours as a toddler. Pray with them. Scare the ghosts away. Just be what they need.

* * *

My prayer for you as you walk away from this book is that you will feel supernatural bravery. That you will believe that you can walk through the tough stuff with more strength than you believe you possess. I pray that you'll learn and actually lean on others. And that you will choose courage, because it is a choice. I pray that you will know that love makes it possible to walk through anything, which is exactly why Jesus died for you.

Lord, may you be with each person who reads this story. May your loving presence in their hardships be evident and the courage that only you are able to bestow be so abundant in their lives. God, show your grace and your mercy in their own stories, and may each person feel an overwhelming sense of love even in the valley of the shadows. Thank you, Lord, for being holy over all, and for loving us in a way that only You can.

ACKNOWLEDGEMENTS

It took even more of a team to get these words on paper than it did to walk through the story you just read.

Adam, I love you forever and a little while. Without your steadfastness, support, and love, this book would not have been written, and we would not have come out of the last seven years intact. You are the best husband, partner, and teammate I could ask for. Thank you for all you do for me and our little family.

Knox and Savannah, thank you for bringing out the best in me. For being patient and understanding as I spent time writing this. You two are my legacy and my greatest joys, and being your mom is my more rewarding job. I love you, I am so proud of you, and I will always be your mom.

I couldn't have done this without the prayer warriors and accountability buddies that are Marites Kliem and Carissa Krause. Your prayers and encouragement are the reason this book both got started and got finished. Thank you.

To Auntie Char—I love you. Thank you for believing in me, encouraging me to follow my call. I want to be like you one day.

I have the best circle of friends and family around me that have read this, encouraged me, and made sure I continued even when I didn't want to. Amber, Gloria, Liz, Kyla, Jayme—I don't know where I would be without you all. Mark, Shelley, Darlee-Ann, Kenton

— thank you for asking the right questions (and bringing tissues) to support me in exactly how I needed it both in the journey, and the writing of this book.

Grace Fatkin, you have always been the little voice in my head that gives me confidence when it comes to my words. As my teacher, mentor, and friend, you have guided me in both my technical craft and my life. Without your mentorship, I would be lost. Thank you.

Tracey Dickie is more than a counsellor; she is a friend. This book is a true product of six years of conversations, tears, and therapy with you. You've made this possible and walked with me through these memories and reflections. Thank you for never giving up on me—and don't think our sessions are over just because I finally got it all out on paper.

I like to pretend I understand all the medical jargon and lingo that I've picked up in the last few years, but it was truly Katie Wiskar who made sense of it all in this book and for me. Katie, you give me courage and truth when I need it. I owe you so much more than I could ever put into words, and I love you.

Robynn Friesen, thank you for being my first-ever reader and for diligently reading each word of this book . . . and then letting me vent about it every day after. Your friendship and loyalty are unparalleled. I'm glad our houses will one day be connected. Thank you.

Laura Matheson, my amazing editor at FriesenPress. You had the unenviable task of "fixing this book," and gosh, I am glad for it. Your thoughtfulness and care are evident in each of the hundreds of comments and every word of our conversations. You are better than a fairy godmother. Thank you.

To the people that have and continue to lift up my family in more ways than I can count, I am endlessly grateful. Cheryl, Perry, Daryl, Janet, Roxie, Orv, Ernie, Laurie: you are more than friends; you are family.

To my biological family that never leaves and always shows up when I need you most, I love you and I am so thankful for your continued presence in my life. This book is a dedication to the strength of our family, across so many provinces. Pam, Becca, and Auntie Irene, thank you especially for your prayers and encouragement when I stalled and needed it most.

The medical teams that handled both Mom and Dad's cases were fantastic. From the paramedics to the nurses, doctors, the rapists (yes, I know I spelled it that way), and support staff. We wouldn't be standing without you. Bailey, thank you for continuing to journey with Dad in a way that only you can.

Kurt and Bonnie, thank you for being my parents. For keeping Mom and Dad's memories alive with your stories and your own memories. Thank you for taking care of me as if I were your own, and for the grace you've shown me as I navigate this journey of grief. I wouldn't be who I am without you two.

Joelle and Robby, thank you for being so supportive and loving through this all. For asking about the project, giving me space when I needed it, and simply just being you. I love you two.

Cody and Carlee, thank you for trusting me with this story. For allowing me to tell my version of what happened all those years ago and for your support through it. I know that being a few provinces away was so challenging, but it never felt like you were far. Your love and sacrifice will never be taken for granted or forgotten. I love you both.

Mom and Dad, you are literally the reason I am here and the reason for this story. I love you, I am so proud of you, and I will always be your daughter.

ABOUT THE AUTHOR

 Rayel Bausenhaus is a former varsity volleyball player, having spent five years with the UBC Thunderbirds women's volleyball team, winning five consecutive national championships. When she's not planning activities and sensory bins for her children, she works as a human resources consultant, specializing in strategy development and implementation within small- and medium-sized businesses.

On her twenty-sixth birthday, right after her wedding, Bausenhaus became a member of the sandwich generation. She received a phone call from the RCMP that her father had had a heart attack while cycling. While he was in one hospital and rehab for the next six months, her mother's cancer returned, and she passed away shortly after. Bausenhaus' goal is to build a community of people walking through the stickiness that is life in the middle of the peanut butter sandwich generation.

In her spare time, Bausenhaus loves to camp, cook new recipes, organize everything she can find, and spend time with her family and friends. She volunteers with a variety of capacities within the sectors of sport, non-profit, and ministry.

Bausenhaus lives in Vancouver, BC, with her husband and their two children.